A Schema Therapy Self-Help Guide to Avoidant Personality Disorder

Easing Shame, Quieting Self-Doubt, and Letting People In

The Quiet Distance Series Book 2

The Self-HelpEdition

Lucius Granville Glenn

This book is intended for general informational and educational purposes only. It is not a substitute for professional medical, psychological, or psychiatric advice, diagnosis, or treatment, and reading it does not create a therapeutic relationship of any kind. If you are concerned about your mental health, please consult a qualified professional.

The author makes no guarantee of any particular outcome. Any application of the ideas and exercises in this book is undertaken at the reader's own discretion and responsibility. Progress varies from person to person, and the material is offered as a starting point rather than a promised result.

All names, characters, examples, and scenarios in this book are fictional or composite. They are drawn from common patterns and are presented for illustration only. They are not intended to depict, identify, harm, or misrepresent any actual person or entity, and any resemblance to a specific individual is unintended.

First edition:2026

ISBN: 978-1-7647265-2-8

Table of Contents

Preface

For all that avoidant personality disorder is among the more common patterns seen in mental health settings, it remains one of the least understood by the people who live with it. Public conversation about anxiety and self-esteem has grown considerably, yet the specific pattern of wanting connection while reliably retreating from it has stayed in the background, rarely named and seldom explained in terms a non-specialist can use. The result is that many people carry this pattern for decades without a clear account of what it is or where it comes from. A guide written plainly, for the person living the experience rather than the professional studying it, has been missing.

This book defines the pattern at its center as a learned strategy organized around a single early belief: that one is, in some hard to specify way, not enough. That belief expresses itself through social inhibition and a steady expectation of rejection. The distinction matters, because this pattern is often confused with two others. It is not the same as situational social anxiety, which centers on fear in particular settings rather than a settled judgment about the self. It is not the same as introversion, which is a preference for solitude rather than a protective retreat from feared exposure. Naming the difference is the first step toward addressing the right thing.

The difficulty most readers face is not a lack of effort but a lack of a map. People living with this pattern often work hard to manage it, frequently by pushing themselves into situations that feel like ordeals, or by criticizing themselves toward a change that criticism cannot produce. What they tend not to have is a structured understanding of the parts that keep the pattern running, and a sense of which steps actually loosen it.

This book applies the schema therapy model in accessible terms. It identifies the core belief, the inner critic that enforces it, the protective wall that keeps others at a distance, and the younger self that learned to hide, then offers practical, paced methods for working with each: self-compassion as a foundation, small experiments in visibility, and the skills to tolerate closeness and repair it after withdrawal. The aim is a gradual widening of the life that avoidance has narrowed.

It has a companion written for clinicians, covering the same model in professional terms. The two are designed to work together, though each stands on its own. This volume is the one written for the person doing the work from the inside, and a reader working with a therapist is welcome to bring its language into that room.

This book speaks directly to readers who recognize the pattern in themselves, and it will also serve partners, family members, and practitioners who want a clear account of it. It is not therapy, it does not diagnose, and it makes no promise of a particular result. Change in this work is a direction held over time rather than a destination reached on a schedule. What this book offers is a clear, usable way to understand a long-standing pattern and to begin, gently and at your own pace, to live less governed by it.

A Note Before You Begin

If you've picked up this book, you may already be carrying something quiet and heavy. The sense that you don't quite belong. That closeness costs more than it should. That you are not, in some hard to name way, enough. I've written what follows for you, with care.

A few things to say up front, so we start from honest ground.

This is a self-help book, not a clinical one. It's written to help you understand a pattern that many people live with, and to walk alongside you as you begin to change it gently, at your own pace. It is not a diagnosis. It is not therapy. Reading it will not make me your therapist, and it will not replace the work that can happen with a qualified professional. If something in here lands hard, or you find yourself struggling more than you can carry, please consider reaching out to a therapist, a doctor, or someone you trust. There is real help available, and asking for it is not a failure of self-help. It's part of it.

You don't have to read this book in order, though I've written it as if you might. Each chapter builds on what came before, but you're welcome to skip a chapter, come back to it, or sit with a section for longer than I expect. Some pages may feel close to the bone. That's okay. Close the book when you need to. The page will wait.

A few small invitations.

Read with kindness. The book is about a part of you that has been criticized enough already. Try not to add to that. If you catch yourself using what you read as fresh evidence against yourself, that is the pattern doing its work, and we'll talk about it.

Try the exercises that interest you and skip the ones that don't. Self-help works best when it is yours, not mine.

Bring patience. The shifts this book is pointing toward are quiet and accumulate slowly. If you feel nothing for the first three chapters and then something small loosens in the fourth, that is the work doing what it does.

This book also has a companion. There is a clinician's edition under the same title, written for therapists. If you're working with someone, they may find it useful. You don't need it to read this one. They are deliberately twinned, but each stands on its own.

One last thing. If, at any point while reading, you find yourself unsafe, in crisis, or thinking of harming yourself, please put the book down and reach out for help. Call a crisis line, contact your doctor, or tell a trusted person what is going on. This book will still be here when you come back. You are worth the call.

Let's begin.

A Short Primer

You don't need to know what schema therapy is to read this book. I will teach you the ideas as we go, in plain words, when each one is needed. But you've picked up a book with schema therapy in the title, and it's fair to want a short answer up front. Here it is.

Schema therapy is a way of understanding why some patterns in our lives keep repeating, even when we know better, even when we want them to stop. It was developed in the 1990s by an American psychologist named Jeffrey Young, who had trained as a cognitive therapist and noticed that the standard methods worked beautifully for many people and not at all for others. The clients who didn't respond were not lazy or resistant. They were carrying something older and more settled, beliefs about themselves that had formed in childhood and had been quietly running the show ever since. Young, along with his colleagues Janet Klosko and Marjorie Weishaar, built a method to address those beliefs directly, drawing on cognitive therapy, attachment ideas, and several experiential approaches (Young et al., 2003). The approach has since been studied and adapted for many long-standing personality and relational patterns, although evidence specific to avoidant personality disorder remains more limited than the broader personality-disorder literature.

There are two words from schema therapy you'll meet again and again. I'd like you to know what they mean now, even if loosely, so that nothing in the chapters that follow lands as jargon.

The first word is *schema*. A schema is an early, deep belief about yourself or the world, formed when you were young, often before you had words for it. Some examples: *I am not safe. I am not lovable. People will leave. My needs are too much.* You did not choose these beliefs. They were learned, often from experiences that made perfect sense to a child trying to understand what was happening around them. The trouble is that a schema doesn't stay where it was learned. It travels with you. It shapes how you read a colleague's tone, how you interpret a silence in a friendship, how you feel when someone says something kind. Long after the original circumstances have changed, the schema is still doing its work.

The schema this book centers on is sometimes called the *defectiveness schema*. In plain words, it is the deep, persistent feeling that you are flawed in some hard to name way, that if people really knew you they would draw back, that you are not, somewhere underneath, enough. If that sentence lands somewhere familiar, you're in the right book.

The second word is *mode*. A mode is a part of you that responds to the schema. Some modes try to protect you from the pain of the belief, often by going quiet, going numb, or going away. Some modes echo the criticism you heard growing up, replaying it in your own voice. Some modes carry the younger you who first learned to hide. And one mode is the steadier, kinder adult voice you are slowly building, the part of you that can hold the others.

You'll meet four of these parts in this book. You will recognize most of them. We'll give them plain names as we go: the part of you that retreats, the inner critic, the younger you who learned to brace, and the steadier you who is doing the reading. Nothing here will be tested. There is no terminology you need to memorize.

What schema therapy adds to the older approaches is two ideas that matter for the work that follows. First, that the old beliefs are not arguments to be won. They were learned in a way that does not yield to logic alone. Reaching them takes a different kind of approach, gentler and more direct, and that approach can be taught. Second, that the parts of you in conflict are not enemies. The protective ones, the critical ones, the wounded ones, all of them developed for a reason. Working with them is, in part, learning what they were trying to do.

That is the whole framework, in two pages. You now know more than enough to begin.

A note before we go on. If you're already in therapy with someone who uses schema therapy or another related approach, this book can sit alongside that work, but it is not a substitute. Tell your therapist what you're reading. Many therapists welcome it. If you are not in therapy and want to be, the final chapter has a careful look at when to consider it and how to find help that fits.

Introduction: The Quiet Distance

Ines stands at the corner of the bar with her coat still on. She's been here ninety seconds. Her colleague's leaving drinks have spilled into the back room of a place near the office, and through the glass she can see her team gathered, drinks in hand, the new manager telling a story Ines cannot hear. Two people laugh.

She'd planned to stay for an hour. She'd told herself this on the train, the way she always tells herself, with a certain firmness, that this time she would. The whole afternoon she'd practiced the small things, a casual thing to say about the project, a question to ask the leaver about her next job, an exit line for when she'd been there long enough. She had everything ready.

What she hadn't planned for was the moment of standing at the corner of the bar, watching the team without yet being seen, and feeling, abruptly, that she had no business being in the room. Not in any way she could articulate. Not because anyone had told her she didn't belong. Just a quiet, settled certainty that her presence would dim the evening by a fraction, and that the fraction would be noticed.

She puts her coat back on. She tells herself she'll say a quick hello and then go. By the time she's crossed the room she's decided not to bother the manager mid-story. By the time she's nodded to two colleagues she's decided not to interrupt the leaver, who is laughing with someone else. She picks up the card she'd brought, signed but not handed over, and slips it onto the table near the gifts. She leaves through the side door because the front door means walking past the group again.

On the train home she replays the version of the evening where she stayed. In that version she said the thing about the project and the manager turned and laughed. In that version someone made room for her at the bar. In that version she went home with the warm feeling of a small inclusion. She knows, with the same quiet certainty, that the actual evening cost nothing visible, that no one will mention her early exit, that no one will think badly of her. She also knows she'll spend the rest of the night wishing she had stayed.

Ines, like the others you'll meet in this book, is a composite. The details are not from any single person. The pattern is from many.

If any part of that scene felt familiar, even in a different setting, this book is for you. What Ines is living, in a small and unremarkable way, is what I want to call the *quiet distance*. Not the loud distance of conflict or rejection, but the steady, almost imperceptible distance that lives inside an otherwise functioning life. The longing for connection and the certainty that you don't deserve it sit side by side, and the certainty almost always wins.

The pattern has a name, and a shape, and a structure. It also has a way out, slow and gentle and entirely within reach. That is the promise of this book, and I want to make it to you directly. You're not just shy. You're not failing at being human. What you are carrying makes complete sense, given what shaped it, and it can change.

A Pattern, Not a Verdict

The first thing to know is that what you are carrying is not a personal verdict. It is a pattern, and patterns can be understood.

In the clinical literature, the most precise term for what we're looking at is *avoidant personality disorder*, sometimes shortened to AVPD. I'll use the words *avoidant pattern* through most of this book, because the diagnostic label, while accurate, carries weight that gets in the way of reading. A label can feel like a verdict when it is meant only as a description. Hear it as a description.

Lampe and Malhi (2018), in a careful review of the current research, describe the core of this pattern as a steady sense of inferiority combined with the constant expectation of rejection, shaping decades of withdrawal across work, friendship, and love. Estimates from large community studies suggest that avoidant personality disorder affects roughly two to three percent of adults, although estimates vary depending on diagnostic method and impairment thresholds (Grant et al., 2004; Trull et al., 2010). It is more common than most people realize, often misread as shyness or social anxiety, and far less well known than the conditions it sits beside. People live with it for years, sometimes their whole lives, without ever being given the language to describe what is happening.

What's happening, in the simplest possible terms, is this. Somewhere along the way, often very young, you learned that being seen was risky. You learned that needs invited disappointment, that warmth could be withdrawn, that being known might mean being judged. You did what any reasonable person would have done with that information. You started to hide. The hiding worked. It got you through. It's still working, in its way, every time you choose the corner of the bar over the group, the side door over the front door, the brief polite version of yourself over the fuller, riskier one. The cost is that you're not, in the deepest sense, in your own life.

The Shape of the Pattern

The pattern shows up in different places for different people. You may recognize yourself in some of these and not others.

It shows up at work. Eloise has good ideas and watches other people present them. She is, by her own account, the most prepared person in most rooms she enters and the least visible. She has not been promoted in five years.

It shows up in friendship. Mateo has known Felix since they were eight. They text twice a year. Mateo writes longer messages to Felix in his head than he ever sends. He told himself last week that he'd call. He didn't call.

It shows up in love. Lucia has ended four relationships before they could find their shape. Each time, the relationship was beginning to feel real. Each time, a quiet voice told her that the other person had not yet seen what was wrong with her, and that staying would only make the eventual departure worse. She left first. Each time, she was sure she was doing them a kindness.

It shows up in ordinary days. Coralie picks the late shift because the lunch break with colleagues feels like too much. Sebastian declines the birthday gathering at the last minute and feels real relief, then a quieter sadness an hour later. Margot opens the dating app, looks at three faces, closes it, opens it again, closes it again.

It shows up in family. Julian doesn't tell his sister about the promotion. He's worried that her excitement, when it comes, will feel like more than he deserves, and that the gap between her reading of him and his reading of himself will widen the conversation past where he can hold it.

These are different people in different lives, but they are not, underneath, doing different things. Look closely and you'll see the same internal sequence in each of them. A moment of potential connection. A flash of expectation that the connection will go badly. A small invisible decision to opt out before the bad thing can happen. The opting out is so well practiced that it does not feel like a decision. It feels like the only sensible response to the situation in front of them. They are all responding to the same belief, which is the next thing to talk about.

The Belief That Runs the Show

If you sat with each of those people long enough, in the right conditions, you'd find roughly the same sentence underneath. It might be worded differently. It might not be conscious. But it's there, and it sounds something like this. *If they really knew me, they wouldn't want me.*

That sentence, or its many cousins, is the engine of the pattern. Schema therapy gives this belief a name, the *defectiveness schema*, but the technical language matters less than the recognition. The defectiveness schema is not a thought you sometimes have. It is a settled, often quiet conviction that lives below your ordinary thinking and shapes what you do with everything that arrives, every compliment, every closeness, every chance to be seen. Compliments get reinterpreted. Closeness gets handled carefully so it cannot end badly. Chances to be seen get refused before they can ask anything of you.

Consider what happens when someone says something kind to you. The defectiveness belief is doing real work in that moment, although you don't see it. The kind sentence reaches you, and somewhere inside, almost instantly, it is processed. *They are being polite. They don't really know me. They would say this to anyone.* The compliment, which was warm when it left the other person's mouth, arrives at you cooled to nothing. You may not even register that this has happened. You only notice that the warmth, oddly, did not land.

Most of the time, you don't notice the belief working. You notice its results. You notice that you chose the corner of the bar. You notice that you didn't send the message. You notice that another year has passed and the friendships you wanted are still acquaintances. The belief itself stays just below the waterline, where it does its work.

Here is the part that is going to matter through the rest of the book. The belief is not the truth about you. It is a sentence you learned, once, from a situation that taught it to you. It feels like the truth because it has been repeating for a long time, and because it has shaped the evidence you've taken from your life in ways that quietly confirm it. People who try to argue with the defectiveness belief head on, with logic, with affirmations, almost always lose. The belief is older than logic. It needs a different kind of work.

The good news, and there is good news, is that this is something you can learn to see. Once you can see it, you can begin to answer it. Once you can answer it, the things you do at the corner of the bar begin to shift. Not all at once. Not overnight. But truly. Schema therapy was built to work with enduring schemas and coping patterns, and a multicenter trial found benefits for several personality disorders, including many cluster-C presentations (Bamelis et al., 2014). The path is promising, but it should be understood as gradual work rather than a guaranteed result.

What This Book Offers

This book takes you through the pattern from the inside out, in five short parts.

In Part One, you'll learn to recognize the pattern in your own life, separate it from things it looks like but is not, name the belief that drives it, and understand, with compassion, where it came from. You didn't choose this. It was learned. And what was learned can be unlearned.

In Part Two, you'll meet the parts of yourself involved in the pattern. The part that goes quiet to protect you. The inner critic that learned its lines from someone else and now uses your own voice. The younger you who first learned to hide. And the steadier you, the one doing the reading, the one this whole book is building.

You'll learn to name these parts as they appear in your life, in real time, so that when the protector engages you can recognize it, when the critic speaks you can answer it, and when the younger you needs comfort you can give it. The work is in the seeing first. The shifting follows.

In Part Three, you'll look at how the pattern plays out in your relationships and in the life you have held back from. Honestly, without judgment, with the aim of seeing clearly rather than feeling worse.

In Part Four, you'll start to change it. Not by forcing yourself into uncomfortable situations as some kind of test. By learning to soften the inner critic, to risk small acts of being seen, to stay close when the urge is to run.

In Part Five, you'll look at how to keep what you have built, what to do when you slip, and how to find professional help if and when you want it. Self-help and therapy are not opposites. They are friends.

You will not be asked to do anything ambitious or fast. Each chapter ends with one small action you can try, if you want to, within the week ahead. Skip the ones that don't fit. Repeat the ones that do.

How to Use This Book

A few practical things.

Read in order if you can. Each chapter builds on the one before. If you read Chapter 9 without Chapter 3, you'll miss some of what makes Chapter 9 useful.

You can also read out of order if you need to. Some chapters touch material that will be harder for some readers than others, particularly Chapter 4, on where this began, and Chapter 7, on the younger you. If those feel like too much on a given day, set them aside. The book will still be here.

Keep a notebook if it helps. Plenty of readers do the exercises in their head and get a great deal out of the book. Others find that writing things down changes how the material lands. Try both. Use what works.

And read kindly. The reading itself can be hard, because the book is about a part of you that has been criticized enough. If you find yourself using what is here as fresh evidence against yourself, notice the pattern doing its work, close the book, and come back when it has loosened.

A First Invitation

I'd like to give you something small to try this week.

In the next seven days, simply notice. Without judgment, without trying to change anything, watch for one moment in which you held back. It might be a message you started and didn't send. A conversation you trimmed shorter than it could have been. A gathering you avoided. A compliment you brushed off. A piece of yourself you decided not to share.

You don't need to do anything different in that moment. You only need to see it.

Then, when it has passed, ask yourself one question, gently. *What did the part of me that held back think it was protecting me from?*

You don't have to have an answer. The question itself, asked kindly, is the work.

In a Nutshell

What you've been living, the longing and the fleeing, the corner of the bar, the message that stays in drafts, is a recognizable pattern with a name and a structure. It's not a flaw in you. It's something you learned, for reasons that made sense at the time. Underneath it sits a quiet belief that says you are not, in some hard to name way, enough. That belief can be seen, can be answered, and over time can loosen its grip. The work is slow, gentle, and entirely within reach. The next chapter is where we begin.

Chapter 1 When Distance Feels Safer

Paloma is eleven days into a new job and she has just declined her third lunch invitation. The first two felt explainable. She'd brought lunch already. She had a call to prep for. The third one she watched herself decline before her brain caught up. Three colleagues, two of whom she liked, asked if she wanted to come along to the place across the street. The word *no* was already in her mouth before they finished the sentence.

She said something about a deadline that wasn't real. They said sure, maybe tomorrow. They left. She sat at her desk with the sandwich she had packed and watched the small group walk past the window. Two of them were laughing. She'd told herself, when she'd accepted this job, that she would try to be more open this time. She had meant it. She had also, eleven days in, declined three invitations she actually wanted.

What she felt afterward was not regret, not exactly. It was something quieter and more familiar. A slight flatness. The sense that she'd done what she usually did, and that the doing of it was so automatic she could not point to the moment of decision. There was no decision. There was just the answer.

If you've ever been Paloma in some version of that scene, you already know what this chapter is about. The pattern this book takes seriously is not a series of dramatic choices to pull back. It's a thousand small moments, most of them invisible to you, in which the answer is already in your mouth before the question has finished arriving. The chapter you're reading now is about learning to see those moments. Not to fix them yet. Just to see them.

Here is the principle that will hold the rest of this book together. What we're going to call *the quiet distance* is not a flaw in your personality. It's a pattern that takes shape in small moments, accumulates over years, and is finally easier to spot once you know what to look for. The first task is not to change it. The first task is to notice it. Recognition is the work of this chapter, and recognition, done with kindness, is the start of every change that follows.

The Pattern in Plain Sight

The patterns we miss are the ones that look like our normal life. If something happens once, you notice it. If it happens five hundred times, it stops being an event and starts being you.

That is the difficulty of the quiet distance. It hides inside the ordinary. The lunch declined. The text not sent. The compliment brushed off. The opportunity not raised. The small piece of yourself withheld from someone who wanted to know you. None of these things looks like a moment of avoidance from the inside. They look like preferences, or pragmatism, or just how you are.

A lot of people live for years inside this pattern without ever giving it a name. They wonder why their friendships stay shallow. They wonder why opportunities seem to find other people. They wonder why warmth from a partner doesn't, somehow, fill in the way it seems to fill other people. They look at the question and find a list of explanations that always points away from the pattern. *I'm just busy. I'm just a private person. The job market is tough. They probably didn't really mean the invitation.*

Each of these explanations might be true in the small case. None of them, on their own, accounts for the shape your life has taken.

The research bears this out. The pattern Lampe and Malhi (2018) describe in their careful review of avoidant personality disorder is striking precisely because it shows up not in a few dramatic episodes but in the texture of an ordinary life. Decades of withdrawal across work, friendship, and love. People functioning at a high enough level that no one around them sees the cost. The cost is paid in private, in a thousand small moments of holding back that never add up to a single story you could tell at a dinner party.

A Quiet Inventory

Let me give you a way to start seeing it.

The exercise that opens this work is not a diagnostic checklist. It's an invitation to notice. Read the situations below slowly. For each one, just notice whether it feels familiar. Don't grade yourself. Don't add it up. Just see what is there.

You go to a gathering where you know one or two people. You spend most of the evening with them and leave earlier than you'd intended.

A friend you used to be close to texts to suggest a meet-up. You read the message. You mean to reply. You don't. A week passes. You feel worse, not better.

Someone says something kind to you. You think, almost instantly, *they don't really mean that, they're just being polite.*

You have an idea in a meeting that you think is good. You watch someone else say something similar, slightly worse, and watch the room respond to them.

You meet someone new whose attention you want. You pull back slightly, to test whether they pull back too, and they do.

Someone close to you asks how you really are. You say fine. You change the subject.

That isn't a quiz. There's no score. But if even three of those situations made something turn slightly in your chest, you're in the right book, and you're reading the right chapter.

This is the work of Chapter 1. Just to see. To gather the data of your own days, gently. The pattern will reveal itself once you stop walking past it.

A Day in the Life of the Pattern

If you wanted to watch the quiet distance work over a single day, here's what it could look like, lightly composited.

Zoe wakes up to a message from a friend. The friend has been meaning to catch up. Zoe reads the message twice. She means to reply. Something pulls her into the morning instead. By lunch she has not replied, and the not-replying has become its own small weight.

At work, a senior colleague stops by her desk and tells her the report she submitted was excellent, the best in the team. Zoe says thank you, smiles politely, and the warmth of the compliment does not, somehow, reach her. Walking back to the meeting room she catches herself rehearsing the reasons the colleague was being generous rather than honest. Five reasons. She is, she notices, very good at this.

In the meeting, an idea forms in her head. It's a real idea. It would help the team. She rehearses how she would say it. Someone else says something close to it, slightly worse. The room responds. Zoe doesn't add the better version.

At lunch she sits with her sandwich at her desk. A colleague passes and waves. Zoe waves back and looks at her screen.

After work she calls her mother. The conversation stays at the level of news, weather, plans. There's a thing Zoe has been thinking about that she would have liked to talk about. She doesn't say it.

Before bed she thinks about the message from her friend. She tells herself she'll reply tomorrow.

None of this is dramatic. None of it would show up in a story she'd tell about her day if someone asked. It would not, in fact, show up to herself, unless she'd been taught to look.

That sketch is composited from several patterns I've seen many times in this work; no single client is in it; every detail in it has shown up in the rooms I've sat in. It's the texture of the quiet distance. It does its work invisibly. Most days, on most lives, the work goes unseen.

Until you start seeing.

What Recognition Does

Recognition is sometimes mistaken for an indictment. It's not. When you start to see the quiet distance in your own life, the part of you that has been criticized enough already will try to use the seeing as fresh evidence. *See. I knew there was something wrong with me. I'm broken in a way I now have proof of.*

That is the pattern, doing the work it has been doing for a long time. It takes new information and makes it into another version of the same sentence. The work of this book, and the work of this chapter, is to learn to recognize the pattern without letting the pattern recruit the recognition.

Recognition, kindly held, does something else. It gives you a place to stand. It moves the thing you're looking at from *who I am* to *what I do*. That move is small in language and large in everything else. *Who I am* cannot be changed. *What I do* can be examined, can be questioned, can over time be done differently.

Marcel, a man in his late forties, told me once that the first month of his work in this area felt like he was being shown a movie he'd been in all his life without ever realizing he was in it. He could see the small moments now. The lunch declined. The conversation trimmed short. The brother he hadn't called back. Seeing the moments did not, at first, change anything. It made him sad. But within three months, the seeing itself began to slow the moments down. The *no* was no longer entirely in his mouth before the question arrived. There was a half-second now, in which something was possible.

That half-second is what recognition does. It's not change. It's the space where change can begin.

Where the Pattern Tends to Live

Across many years of this work, I've noticed that the quiet distance tends to settle into a small number of places in a given life. Most people find that they hold back most reliably in two or three settings, while moving more freely in others. Knowing where the pattern lives most in your own life is one of the more useful things this chapter can give you.

Some people hold back most at work. They have ideas they don't raise, projects they don't volunteer for, conflicts they avoid by going quiet. Clara has been at her company for eleven years and is the most knowledgeable person on her team. Her manager has told her, twice, that she should be more visible. She nods, and stays in her lane. The cost shows up in a flat career, and in the colleagues hired three years after her who now sit a level above.

Some hold back most in friendships. They have a wide acquaintanceship and few close friends. They are present at events and absent from the ones that would have taken effort. Hugo has six friends he likes very much, all of whom would call themselves close to him. Hugo would call himself close to none of them. He hasn't suggested a meet-up first in eight years.

Some hold back most in romantic relationships. They find connection, and then, just before it becomes real, they pull back. They convince themselves the other person was wrong for them. They leave first. Lucia, who we'll meet again in a later chapter, has ended four relationships in eight years. Each time, the relationship was beginning to feel real. Each time, she was sure she was being honest with herself about a mismatch she'd suddenly seen. Each time, the mismatch she'd suddenly seen looked, on later inspection, exactly like the moment things got close.

Some hold back most with family. They are the cordial one, the polite one, the one who keeps things light. The deeper conversations that other family members have stayed up for don't seem to find them. They make sure of that. Sebastian sees his sister three times a year and has had, in his recollection, no real conversations with her since they were teenagers. He would say they're close. He has not told her about the diagnosis he received last spring.

And some hold back most in the ordinary moments. The neighbor not greeted. The hairdresser not chatted with. The barista's name they could remember and don't. A life lived at a half-step from the world.

Most readers find themselves in two or three of those, with one usually more dominant than the others. Pay attention to which ones move you. You'll need that information in a few chapters.

A First Action

I want you to try something small this week.

For the next seven days, look for a single moment of holding back. Not a dramatic one. The smaller and more ordinary the better. The text not sent. The thing you almost said. The smile not returned. The compliment deflected. The invitation declined before you'd thought about it.

When you spot one, do nothing different. Don't push yourself to override it. Don't promise yourself you'll do better next time. Just notice.

Then, when the moment has passed and the small ache has settled, ask yourself one gentle question. *What did the part of me that pulled back think it was protecting me from?*

You don't need to have a clean answer. You don't have to have any answer at all. The question, asked kindly, is the work.

A few readers find it useful to keep a small notebook for the week. A line or two per noticing. That isn't required. The watching is what matters.

What Recognition Is Not

Two more things before we close.

Recognition isn't diagnosis. Reading this chapter doesn't mean you have avoidant personality disorder, the clinical name for the deeper version of this pattern. AVPD is a clinical condition estimated in community studies at roughly two to three percent of adults, with rates varying by diagnostic rules and study design (Grant et al., 2004; Lampe & Malhi, 2018; Trull et al., 2010). Many more people carry softer versions of the pattern. Whether the label fits you or not, the work of this book is the same. You don't need a diagnosis to need what's here.

Recognition is also not the same as being able to do anything about the pattern yet. Don't expect yourself to. Some readers, in this first chapter, get a sudden burst of resolve and try to override every avoidance for a week. That isn't change. That's the inner critic in a new outfit. The change this book is pointing toward is quieter, slower, and more durable. It starts with seeing. Don't skip the seeing.

In a Nutshell

The quiet distance is a pattern that hides inside ordinary days. It shows up in moments so small you'd never notice them as moments. The first work is not to fix it. It's to see it. Recognition is the first kindness, and it's the only kindness that opens the door to the rest. When you spot a small holding back this week, just see it, gently, and ask what the part of you that pulled back thought it was protecting you from. The answer can come slowly. The seeing is the start.

Chapter 2 More Than Shyness

Hugo is at his oldest friend's fortieth birthday party. He's been there an hour and has spoken to four people, all of them friends of the friend. He's been polite. He's smiled at the right moments. He's also been counting the minutes until the cake, because the cake means people stop circulating for ten minutes and he can stand quietly in the corner with a slice of it and not have to explain himself.

A cousin of the birthday friend, a kind woman in her fifties whom Hugo has met before, finds him by the kitchen island. She knows Hugo is *the shy one*, as the friend has affectionately called him for fifteen years. She gives him a small, well-meaning speech. *Just be yourself, Hugo. Nobody is watching you. Everybody here is too busy worrying about themselves to think about you.* She pats his arm. She moves on.

Hugo nods. He smiles. He feels worse.

He feels worse because the cousin's advice, which would have worked perfectly for a different kind of person, doesn't fit the problem he's actually carrying. The cousin thinks Hugo is worried about looking awkward. Hugo isn't. Hugo could look awkward all night and be fine. What Hugo is worried about, although he wouldn't say it this clearly, is being seen. The cousin's advice solves the wrong problem.

If you've ever received the *just be more confident* speech from a kind person and walked away feeling more, not less, alone, this chapter is for you.

Here is the principle. Shyness is about how you appear. The pattern this book takes seriously is about what you believe is underneath the appearance. They look identical from the outside and are completely different inside. Telling someone with the deeper pattern to *be more confident* is like telling someone with a broken leg to walk more cheerfully. The pep talk addresses the wrong layer.

Shyness Is a Volume Knob

Shyness, in plain terms, is a temperament. It means that being the center of attention feels uncomfortable, that meeting new people takes a bit of warm-up, that you'd rather speak after you've watched the room for a while. Shyness wants the same things other people want, which is mostly to be liked and to belong, but it wants those things at a lower volume than other people. The shy person doesn't avoid connection. They just take longer to settle into it.

Most shy people, if you give them time and a safe enough setting, are good at being known. They have warm friendships. They have romantic relationships that look like everyone else's. They have ordinary social lives, with the volume turned down a notch. They get better at parties with practice, the way most people get better at parties with practice.

The pattern this book takes seriously doesn't get better with practice in the same way. People with the deeper pattern can go to a hundred parties and not feel meaningfully more at home in the hundred-first. The reps don't compound. That is one of the cleanest tells that something else is going on. Shyness improves with exposure. The quiet distance doesn't, on its own.

The Introvert Who Is Not You

A similar distinction matters with introversion.

Elio is an introvert. He works in a job he likes and lives in a small flat. He has three close friends he sees regularly and a partner he loves. He doesn't enjoy big gatherings, doesn't pursue them, and when he goes to one, he leaves early without much fuss. After a long day of socializing, he needs a quiet evening to recover. None of this troubles him. He is, by any reasonable measure, happy.

Elio is not the reader of this book.

Introversion is a preference for less stimulation, processed alone or with a small number of people. Introverts can be very social, in their own way. They are not lonely. They aren't hiding. They aren't waiting for someone to find them. They have what they want, in the doses they want it.

The quiet distance looks like introversion from the outside. The avoider goes home early too. The avoider doesn't enjoy big gatherings either. The difference is what the avoider feels afterward.

Try this distinction. After a quiet evening, the introvert feels restored. After a quiet evening that should have been a connection, the avoider feels a small, specific loneliness that doesn't have a name. The introvert chose the quiet. The avoider was chosen by it.

If that small loneliness is familiar, you are probably not, underneath, an introvert. You are probably someone using the language of introversion to make sense of a pattern that runs deeper.

Why the Wrong Advice Has Felt Wrong

If you've been reading self-help books for years and finding them either useless or briefly motivating, the explanation in this chapter is worth sitting with.

Most popular advice for people who hold back assumes the problem is the volume of you. Speak up more. Take up more space. Believe in yourself. Walk taller. The advice works fine if the underlying belief is that you are roughly fine and just need a louder version of yourself in the world.

The advice doesn't work, and tends to make people feel worse, if the underlying belief is that you are not, in some hard to name way, all right. In that case, every push to be louder is read by the part of you that's been hiding as a push to make yourself a bigger target. You're being told to make sure the thing you've been hiding is more visible. Of course you don't take the advice. Of course the courses don't stick.

Hugo, the man at the birthday party, had been on three different confidence courses over the previous decade. He'd liked each one for about a week. Then the small voice that had run his social life since he was nine would quietly disqualify the new behaviors. *That was forced. That wasn't really you. You sounded like an idiot.* The advice had been built for someone whose problem was speaking up. Hugo's problem wasn't speaking up. The advice never reached him.

This isn't your failure. The advice was the wrong medicine for the condition. Better matched help exists, and the rest of this book is one version of it.

Social Anxiety, and What's Underneath

The closest cousin to the pattern we're talking about is social anxiety.

Social anxiety is, roughly, a strong, specific fear of being negatively judged in social situations. It includes fear of looking nervous, of saying the wrong thing, of being embarrassed. People with social anxiety can describe what they are afraid of. They know it's specific. They often know it's, in some sense, more intense than the situation warrants.

The trouble is that AVPD and social anxiety look like each other, and the research has been arguing for years about whether they are distinct conditions or two points on the same spectrum (Tillfors et al., 2004). For practical purposes, here is the difference most clinicians and readers find useful.

Social anxiety is mostly about performance. *They'll see me sweat. They'll notice my hands shake. I'll say something stupid.*

The pattern this book is about is mostly about identity. *They'll see what I am. They'll see what's wrong with me. They'll see what I've been hiding.*

That is a different fear. It runs deeper than performance. It does not get fixed by getting better at performances. You can learn to give an excellent speech and still feel, walking home, that they have not yet seen who you really are, and that when they do, the room will quiet.

Many readers carry both. The two patterns sit comfortably together; the social anxiety often forms a public crust over the deeper identity-level belief. Working on the social anxiety can help, and often does. It just won't reach the layer below.

Noemi spent her late twenties working through a structured course of cognitive behavioral therapy for social anxiety. She did the exposures. She gave the speeches that terrified her. She role-played the difficult conversations. By the end of the course, the visible anxiety had dropped considerably. She could give a presentation without her voice shaking. She could meet new people without her hands going cold.

She also noticed, six months later, that the quieter thing she'd carried before the course had not moved. The new colleague she'd hit it off with hadn't, somehow, become a closer friend. The promotion she could now plausibly compete for hadn't, somehow, attracted her ambition. The dating apps she could now open without dread had not, somehow, led anywhere she'd let go to a real beginning.

The CBT had been excellent work for what it had been designed to do. It had reached the performance layer. It had not been built to reach the identity layer, and so it hadn't.

If you have done good work on a related pattern, like social anxiety, and found that the deeper feeling did not move, this is not because you failed at the work. It is because the work you did was solving a real but different problem. The work this book is about is for the layer underneath.

A Respectful Note on Autistic Difference

Some readers will come to this book having recently wondered about themselves and autism, especially if they grew up undiagnosed or were diagnosed late.

Autistic difference is something else again. It's not a pattern that began as protection. It's a neurotype, a different way of perceiving and processing the social world, present from birth. Many autistic adults, particularly those who learned to camouflage their differences to fit in, carry exhaustion and shame that can look from the outside like an avoidant pattern (Hull et al., 2017). Many autistic adults report earlier psychiatric diagnoses they later perceived as misdiagnoses before receiving an autism diagnosis (Kentrou et al., 2024).

I will not, in two paragraphs, do justice to autistic experience. What I will say is this. If you are autistic, or wondering whether you might be, the pattern this book is about may still be present in your life, but it may also be that what looks like the quiet distance from the outside is, for you, the cost of years of masking. The two need to be teased apart, gently, often with help. If that paragraph is your paragraph, please consider working with someone who knows both the schema therapy material and autistic experience well. The right help is out there.

This chapter is not asking you to decide which label fits you. It is asking you to notice whether the feel of the pattern, from the inside, matches the description.

Is It Preference, or Is It Protection

Here is the reflection that makes the most of this chapter.

When you skip a gathering, decline an invitation, leave early, hold back a message, or trim a conversation short, ask yourself one question. *Is this a preference, or is this a protection?*

A preference feels like a choice. You are doing something you actually want to do. The skipping is a small expression of who you are. You wake up the next morning lighter for having honored it.

A protection feels like a closing-down. You are doing something that keeps you safer from something the situation might have asked of you. The skipping is a small piece of self-management. You wake up the next morning slightly heavier, with a residue of something you can't quite name.

The two feel different from the inside, if you slow down enough to notice.

Try the question this week, the next three or four times you find yourself pulling back from something. *Is this preference, or is this protection?* Don't try to override the answer if it comes back as protection. The work is just to know.

Here is what the question can look like in real time. A friend invites you to a Saturday lunch. Your first instinct is to decline. The instinct is so familiar that it almost answers on its own. Now slow the moment down. If this is a preference, you'd want to be at home that Saturday for some reason that has nothing to do with the lunch. You have a project you're excited about. You're tired and you need quiet. You actually don't enjoy lunches in groups, and it's a Tuesday-coffee kind of friend. The lunch isn't yours. That's a real preference.

If this is a protection, you'd want to go and you'd be planning not to. The decline is keeping you safer from something the lunch might have asked of you. Being seen by people who'd remember you next time. Saying things that might be misheard. Feeling, at some point in the afternoon, that the group had moved on to a conversation you weren't quite in. That isn't a preference. That's a small protection, doing its work.

You don't have to override the protection if you spot it. The point of the question is to know. Even just knowing changes the feel of the day.

Name One Belief

I want one more small action from you before we close the chapter.

Pick one belief you have always taken as fact about yourself socially. Something like *I'm just not a people person. I'm too quiet to lead. I'm not interesting enough to keep someone's attention. I'm the kind of person who'd rather be alone.*

Now write the belief down somewhere you'll see it again. Don't try to argue with it. Don't try to replace it. Just write it down.

What you've written is, almost certainly, not a fact. It is a sentence you learned somewhere, repeated long enough that it stopped sounding like a sentence and started sounding like the truth. The next chapter is about the deepest version of that sentence, the one that runs the show in this pattern. Knowing your own surface version of it now will help when we go deeper.

Keep the page. We will look at it again in the next chapter. The sentence you wrote down today is going to be useful when we look at the belief underneath it. Don't lose it, and don't tidy it up between now and then.

In a Nutshell

Shyness wants the spotlight at a lower wattage. Introversion is content with less of it. Social anxiety fears the spotlight will catch you sweating. The pattern this book is about fears the spotlight will catch what you actually are. They look similar from the outside and are completely different inside. The advice that works for shyness doesn't reach this layer. Don't take the failure of that advice as further evidence that something is wrong with you. The advice was solving the wrong problem. The work that will reach the right problem is what the rest of the book is about, and you have already started by reading this far with the honesty and patience it has asked of you. Both qualities will matter more in the chapters ahead than any technique.

Chapter 3 The Belief That Runs the Show

Clara's partner says, on a quiet Sunday morning over coffee, that he is glad he met her. He says it without preamble, the way people sometimes say true things. He looks at her when he says it.

Clara feels, in the half-second after the sentence lands, three things in quick sequence.

The first thing is a small warmth, like the start of a smile, somewhere just under her sternum.

The second thing is a doubt. *He's just saying that. He's in a good mood. It's been a nice morning.*

The third thing is a slow, settling cool, in which the warmth has been explained away and a small, specific tiredness has taken its place. She smiles at him. She says *me too.* The morning continues.

If you had asked her at the time what had just happened, she would have said nothing happened. He said something kind. She felt the kindness. She said something kind back. A nice exchange between two people who love each other.

Something else happened underneath the nice exchange. A sentence that has been running underneath Clara's life for as long as she can remember stepped in to handle the compliment. The sentence is short. It does not announce itself. It is so familiar that Clara could not, in that moment, have said it out loud. It runs like this. *If he really knew me, he wouldn't say that.*

The compliment was warm when it left his mouth. By the time it reached her, it had been cooled to nothing.

This chapter is about that sentence.

Here is the principle. Underneath the quiet distance sits one belief, often in your own voice but learned somewhere long ago, that you are not, in some hard to name way, enough. Schema therapists call it the *defectiveness schema*. You can call it whatever you like. The point is that it is the engine of the pattern. Once you can see it, you can begin to answer it. You can't answer what you can't see.

The Sentence Most People Carry

The defectiveness belief comes in many wordings, but the wordings cluster.

If they really knew me, they wouldn't want me.

I'm fundamentally different from other people, in a bad way.

There's something wrong with me that I can't name and can't fix.

I have to hide what I am to keep what I have.

Other people belong. I get to visit.

The closeness I'm getting is a mistake they haven't caught yet.

If any of those sentences felt familiar, you've already done some of the work of this chapter. If none of them did but a slightly different sentence rose up instead, write that one down. It is the version that is running in you.

The belief is rarely conscious in adult life. Most people who carry it would describe themselves not as believing they are defective but as being realistic about their limitations. The defectiveness belief is excellent at disguising itself as realism. It is the lens you have been looking through for so long that you have forgotten you are wearing it. You think the colors of the world look like that. They don't. You're wearing tinted glasses you can't see.

Schema therapy was built around the idea that beliefs like this one form early, settle in deep, and survive long after the circumstances that taught them have changed (Young et al., 2003). They survive precisely because they are below the reach of ordinary thinking. You can't argue with them in the way you'd argue with a thought, because they aren't thoughts. They are the floor under the thoughts.

How the Belief Reinterprets a Compliment

We just saw what the belief does to a compliment in Clara's morning. Let me name the move clearly, because once you can name it you can spot it.

A compliment arrives. The defectiveness belief, working quietly, evaluates the compliment for fit with its own picture of you. The compliment doesn't fit. Something must, therefore, explain it. The mind, helpful as ever, produces an explanation. *They're being polite. They don't really know me. They're saying this to everyone. They want something. They're in a good mood. They're mistaken.*

The explanation is offered to consciousness as though it were a sober observation. The compliment, now explained, no longer threatens the picture.

Compliments arrive cooled.

This happens hundreds of times a year for some readers. Almost every warm thing said to you is, in fractions of a second, reinterpreted into something colder. You don't decide to do this. You don't notice you are doing this. You only notice that warmth, for you, doesn't seem to fill the way it apparently does for other people. There's an explanation for that.

How the Belief Reinterprets Success

Oscar gets the promotion he has wanted for two years. The promotion is real, well-earned, and confirmed by three different people whose opinions he respects. For two days he feels, with effort, a small pleasure. By the third day, a familiar quietness has set in. He has begun to rehearse the explanation. *They were running out of options. The other candidate said no. It's a smaller team than I thought; it's not a real promotion. They'll see, in six months, that they've made a mistake.*

A friend who has watched Oscar's career congratulates him. He thanks her. Walking home, he thinks she sounded a little tentative, as though she didn't fully believe in the promotion either.

She wasn't tentative. The defectiveness belief was running interference. It does the same thing with success that it does with compliments. It cools the warmth before it can land. Oscar's promotion has been quietly converted, in his head, into something smaller, less real, more temporary. By the end of the week he will be living in a slightly diminished version of his own achievement, and he will not know that he is the one diminishing it.

How the Belief Reinterprets Warmth

Valeria has been friends with the same circle of women since university. They are, by any normal measure, her people. They text her on her birthday. They include her in plans without being asked. They tell her, occasionally, that they love her.

Valeria has, for years, held a quiet conviction that they keep her around mostly out of habit. She would not have said this out loud. She'd have called it being realistic.

The defectiveness belief reads ordinary closeness as a thing she is getting away with rather than a thing she is genuinely receiving. Every warm message is, on its journey from screen to heart, slightly downgraded. The downgrading is so consistent that the warmth never quite settles into the felt sense that she is loved.

That is what the belief does at scale, across years, in a life. It is not, in any single moment, a dramatic event. It is a slow leak in the place where warmth would otherwise pool.

How the Belief Reinterprets an Opportunity

The belief also handles opportunity quietly, the same way it handles compliments.

Gabriel is invited to give a talk at a small conference in his field. The invitation is genuine, from organizers who chose him deliberately. Within an hour of receiving it, Gabriel has produced an internal explanation that brings the invitation back down to scale. *They were probably hard up for speakers. The slot they offered is the small room. Someone else must have dropped out.* By the next morning, the invitation has been quietly recategorized in his mind from *opportunity I deserved* to *opportunity I will need to be careful not to look bad in.*

The recategorization isn't a mistake. The recategorization is the belief doing its protective work. If the invitation is real, then accepting it carries the risk of being seen at something the belief insists you shouldn't be doing. If the invitation is a fluke, then accepting it is humbler, and being seen poorly carries less stake. The belief prefers the second framing because it's safer for the belief itself. The cost is borne by Gabriel, who will give a smaller talk than he could have given, and who will spend the week before it bracing for an audience that is not, in fact, planning to find him out.

If a friend told you they'd received Gabriel's invitation, you would not, instinctively, hand them his interpretation. You would say it sounded like real recognition. You would, in fact, be right.

The Lens, Not the Thought

Here is what I want you to understand most clearly from this chapter.

The defectiveness belief is not a thought you sometimes have. If it were, you could probably argue with it. You'd have noticed it. You would have asked yourself for evidence, and the evidence would have moved you, the way evidence does.

It is a lens. It does not appear in your thinking. It shapes everything that arrives before your thinking ever gets to it. By the time you are conscious of a compliment, a success, or a warm moment, the lens has already worked on it. What you experience consciously is what's left.

This is why people with this pattern try, and fail, to talk themselves into feeling better. *He really did mean it. I should accept the compliment. I should let it in.* The conscious mind has the right idea. But the lens already filtered the moment, and the conscious mind is working with a downgraded copy of the original.

Reaching the lens itself takes a different kind of work. It is gentler, slower, and more direct than argument. We will start that work now and continue it across the next several chapters. Schema therapy research supports work with enduring schemas and coping modes, but the strongest trial evidence cited here is for personality disorders broadly rather than this book's exact self-help format (Bamelis et al., 2014). The lens can shift. It takes time. It is real.

A note for readers who are wondering whether the lens is real for them or whether they are just having ordinary moments of self-doubt. Everyone has self-doubt. Self-doubt is the noisy thing that shows up before a big presentation, a hard conversation, a new social setting. It is loud, it is name-able, it visits and leaves. You can usually recognize it for what it is, even when it has you in its grip.

The defectiveness belief is quieter than self-doubt. It does not get loud before a presentation. It does not announce itself before a date. It works steadily, underneath, on everything that arrives. People with the defectiveness belief usually also have ordinary self-doubt. But it is the steady underneath thing that does the real shaping. If you have ever, after a clearly successful evening, gone home with a small flat feeling rather than a glow, the lens was running. The glow had been intercepted before it could land.

Tell the difference like this. Self-doubt has a topic. The defectiveness belief has a temperature. Self-doubt says *I might mess this up.* The defectiveness belief sets the room a little cooler around everything, all the time. If you can recognize the temperature, you have a name for what you've been moving through, even when you couldn't point to a thought.

Catching the Belief in Your Own Words

Here is the action for this chapter, in two parts.

First, this week, listen for the sentence the belief is using inside you. It will not announce itself. You will catch it sideways, in the moments after a small warmth has somehow not landed. Listen for the explanation your mind produced. The explanation is the belief talking.

Write down the sentence in your own voice. Write the actual words. Not *I have low self-esteem*, which is a textbook phrase. The actual sentence. *He's just being polite. I'm not really good at this. They keep me around out of habit. I don't belong here.* Whatever your version is.

Don't tidy it. Don't argue with it. Just get it onto a page.

Here is what catching looked like, after some practice, for Clara. The next time her partner said something warm to her over coffee, she felt the same three-step sequence we walked through at the start of the chapter. The warmth, the doubt, the cool. This time, she stayed with the doubt for an extra half-second. She caught the actual sentence the doubt was using. *He's saying that because he doesn't know what I'm really like in the mornings.* She wrote the sentence down later that day, in a notebook she'd started keeping. She did not, in that moment, try to change anything else. She just had the sentence on a page in her own handwriting for the first time.

That was the start. The sentence stopped being a lens she couldn't see and became something a little more like a sentence. Sentences can be looked at. Lenses can't.

Reading It as a Friend's Sentence

Second, when you have the sentence written down, read it once more, but read it as though a friend you love had said it about themselves. Read it slowly.

Notice what happens in you when you read it that way.

Most readers, doing this for the first time, feel a small ache and a quick rise of protectiveness on behalf of the imaginary friend. *That isn't true. That's far too harsh. You're being unfair to yourself.* The protectiveness arrives without effort, because for someone you love, the kindness is automatic.

That protectiveness is the first counter-voice you'll learn to use. Right now, you don't need to direct it at yourself. You only need to notice that it exists. You have a kinder voice. You use it on other people all the time. The work of the next several chapters will be helping you turn that voice, gradually, in the other direction.

This is also why the change this book is pointing toward is slow. The kinder voice has to be allowed in at the same speed it was kept out. Forcing it forward feels false to the part of you that learned not to trust it. Letting it come at its own pace works better.

In a Nutshell

Underneath the quiet distance sits one sentence, learned long ago, often in your own voice now. It says you are not, in some hard to name way, enough. It is not a thought you have. It is a lens that filters everything that arrives before your thinking ever sees it. Compliments arrive cooled. Successes are downgraded. Warmth doesn't pool. Reaching the lens takes a different kind of work, gentler than argument. The first move is to catch the sentence in your own words and read it as though someone you love had said it about themselves. The kindness you'd give them is the kindness you'll learn, slowly, to give yourself. The next chapter is about where the sentence came from, and why a child would have learned to say it in the first place.

Chapter 4 Where It Began

Before we go any further, a note about this chapter.

The material in this chapter touches on childhood, on the moments and atmospheres that shape the belief we just named. For most readers, it will be the most emotional chapter so far. That can be useful. It can also be, on some days, more than you came here for. Read it at the pace that suits you. Put it down when you need to. If reading about childhood brings up something heavy that doesn't settle on its own, please consider talking it through with a therapist or someone you trust. This chapter is not asking you to do trauma work alone. It is asking you to look, gently, at where the sentence began.

It is also not asking you to blame anyone. That part matters and we'll come back to it.

Here is the chapter's principle. The defectiveness belief was learned, often very early, in a small thousand moments in which a child concluded, reasonably, given the data available, that the safest move was to hide. That child was not weak. That child was paying attention. Understanding the origin doesn't fix the belief, but it loosens its hold, because once you can see where it came from, it stops looking like the truth about you and starts looking like what it actually is. A conclusion drawn by a younger you, doing their best.

How a Schema Forms

Let me put the technical idea in plain language, because the rest of this chapter rests on it.

Children form working theories about themselves and the world the way scientists form working theories about anything else. They notice. They generalize. They draw conclusions from the patterns in front of them. If the data they have is *needs get met when expressed*, they grow up with a working theory that needs are safe to express. If the data they have is *needs are met sometimes, ignored sometimes, punished sometimes*, they grow up with a different working theory. If the data is *needs are too much*, they grow up with one different again.

The working theory becomes a schema. The schema is the silent floor of the inner life. It doesn't get tested in adulthood, because by then it isn't experienced as a theory. It is experienced as the way things are. Schema therapy was developed to address early maladaptive schemas and coping patterns that often persist despite more present-focused work (Young et al., 2003). The defectiveness schema, the one we're looking at, almost always forms in childhood.

It usually forms not from a single dramatic event but from a steady weather. The phrase that fits this best is the schema therapy phrase *unmet needs*. A child has core needs, things like to be safely held, to have their feelings taken seriously, to be liked for what they are rather than for what they perform, to be allowed to be a child. When those needs go unmet often enough, the child writes a small explanation. *The trouble must be with me.*

That explanation is the start.

The Hiding That Worked

A child who learned to hide was not weak. That child was, in the moment, brilliant.

Children have very few options for handling a world in which their needs aren't safely met. They can't leave. They can't fix the adults. They can't, mostly, even understand what is happening. What they can do is read the room and adjust. They can become smaller. They can become less. They can become whatever the room is willing to tolerate. The hiding is a child's solution to a problem they didn't make.

Felix grew up in a household in which his father, a man under enormous work pressure, would come home tense and need a quiet, low-demand evening. Felix learned by the time he was six that needs raised in the wrong hour made things worse. By eight, Felix had largely stopped raising needs. By twelve, he had largely stopped noticing he had them. His mother told visitors he was *such an easy child*. He was. He had figured out how to be easy. The figuring had cost him more than anyone could see.

That hiding worked, in the only sense that matters when you're eight. It got Felix through. It produced an *easy child* who was praised for not being trouble. The trouble was that the strategy that worked at eight kept working at eighteen and at twenty-eight, when it was no longer needed and now stood between Felix and most of what he wanted. The strategy didn't know that, though. Strategies don't update on their own.

If you carry the quiet distance, somewhere in your past there was a small genius who figured out how to make themselves quieter to stay safer. Don't mock that small genius. Don't try to argue them out of their original solution. Thank them, on your way past. They were doing remarkable work with the materials they had.

Not About Blame

A line that needs saying clearly.

Understanding where the belief came from is not the same as deciding that someone was at fault.

Some readers, looking back at childhoods that taught them to hide, will find clear and serious harm. Others will find a mix of love and limitation, parents who did their best in difficult circumstances and got some of it right and some of it wrong. Many will find a childhood that looked, from the outside, perfectly fine, and contained the steady weather that taught the lesson anyway.

This book is not in the business of helping you build a case against the people who raised you. That is not what the work is for. The work is to see clearly what was learned, so that what was learned can begin to be unlearned. The clearer your seeing, the more you can hold both the love and the limitations of where you came from at the same time. The people who raised you were also raised. The weather around them was made of the weather they grew up in. Tracing the line back too far is exhausting and not particularly useful.

It is also worth saying clearly. For some readers, the childhood that taught the lesson included real harm. Neglect. Cruelty. Forms of contempt that no child should have had to make sense of. If that's your childhood, the work is not to soften what happened or to find sympathetic explanations for the people who did it. The work is to see clearly enough that the belief no longer feels like the truth about you. The harm was real. The belief is also real. They are connected. They are not the same thing. Naming the harm honestly is sometimes the start of being able to put the belief down.

For other readers, the childhood that taught the lesson was loving in most ways and limited in specific ones. There was nothing in particular to point to. The lesson arrived by atmosphere. Both kinds of childhood teach the defectiveness belief. Neither version is more valid. The pattern in your adult life is the pattern, whether it was taught loudly or quietly.

What is useful is this. You did not choose the schema. You were a child. The schema arrived by way of a real situation that you adapted to brilliantly. What is asking to be changed now is not anyone's blame, including yours. It is just the belief that no longer fits the life you are trying to live.

The Messages That Got Through

The defectiveness belief is built from small messages, more than from big events.

Some readers were told, in so many words, that they were too much, too needy, too sensitive, too quiet, too odd. The message arrived through actual sentences. They remember the sentences. The sentences still ring.

Many more readers received the message without anyone saying it out loud. Margot's mother, a kind, depressed woman who couldn't always be reached, communicated something to Margot every time she didn't respond. The message wasn't *you don't matter*. The message was that *whatever Margot was bringing was, in that moment, not bringable*. Repeated across years, the message taught the lesson.

Some readers received the message through comparison. A sibling who was bright in a different way, a cousin who was charming in a way that made the family laugh, a peer at school who got the attention. The lesson wasn't taught by a person being cruel. It was taught by the steady accumulation of evidence that other people moved through the world more easily than the reader did.

Some received it through silence. There was nothing wrong, exactly. There was just no one available to mirror back to them that what they were, in its specific particular form, was welcome. The absence of the mirror taught its own lesson.

Some received it through being misnamed. Coralie grew up in a family that was warm and busy and had no real vocabulary for inner life. When she was sad, an adult would tell her she was tired.

When she was angry, an adult would tell her she was hungry. When she was frightened, an adult would laugh affectionately and tell her she was being dramatic. Nobody was trying to harm her. They named what they could see; they had not been taught the rest. Coralie grew up not knowing what her own feelings were called, because the names she'd been given for them, year after year, hadn't matched. By her twenties, she had a quiet, settled sense that there was something off about how she felt, something not quite legitimate. She couldn't have said why. The lesson had arrived through the steady mismatch between her inner state and the words the people who loved her had used for it.

The form the message took matters less than the result. The result was the sentence we named in the last chapter. *There is something about me that won't, in the long run, be acceptable.*

A Gentle Timeline

Here is the exercise for this chapter. Treat it gently.

Take a piece of paper, or open a blank document. Draw a single horizontal line. At the left end, write *age five*. At the right end, write *now*.

Now, slowly, mark on the line three or four moments in which you remember learning, in some form, that you should be smaller, quieter, less, hidden. These don't have to be dramatic moments. They can be small. A look on a face. A sentence overheard. A holiday when something was off and no one named it. A teacher who treated you with a coolness you couldn't explain. A friendship that ended and never got addressed. A version of yourself you put away because it didn't go down well.

Don't try to write everything down. Three or four is enough. Don't write the moments out in detail. A short phrase per mark is fine.

When you have the marks on the line, sit with the picture for a minute. Don't try to do anything with it. Just look at it.

What you are looking at is the rough shape of where the lesson got taught. It will not be the whole story. There are moments you have forgotten and atmospheres you cannot point to. But the marks you can name give you, for the first time, a kind of evidence in your hand. Evidence that this isn't something innate. Evidence that something was learned, in particular places, by a younger you who was paying attention.

Most readers, doing this for the first time, feel two things at once. A small relief that there is a shape at all, that the belief did not come from nowhere, that it had causes a child responded to. And a small grief, on behalf of that child, that the causes were what they were. The relief and the grief sit side by side. Both belong. You don't have to pick one. You don't have to do anything with either of them today. Let them be what they are. They are the feelings of someone seeing their own story honestly for the first time.

If the exercise feels too much, stop. There is no requirement to finish it today. You can come back to it next month. The line will still be there.

A First Sentence to the Younger You

Here is the second action.

Find a quiet moment. Picture the youngest version of yourself you can clearly remember. Don't picture them in distress. Picture them in a neutral moment. Sitting somewhere. Doing something they liked.

Now, in your head or on paper, say one kind sentence to that child.

You were doing your best.

It wasn't your fault.

I see how hard you were trying.

You weren't too much. You were exactly right.

I'm here now.

Choose whichever sentence rises up. Don't force it. If you can't get one to come, write the simplest version. *I see you.* That is enough.

You may feel something when you do this. A tightening in the throat. A sudden water in the eyes. That is not the work going wrong. That is the part of you we'll be visiting more carefully later in the book, the part that is, in a sense, still waiting for that sentence. If the feeling gets bigger than you can comfortably hold, set the exercise down. It will keep.

When This Is Too Much

A short, plain note before the close.

For some readers, looking at childhood, even at this level, will bring up things that don't easily settle. If that is you, please do not try to push through alone. The work this chapter is touching is the work that is genuinely better done in company. A therapist who knows schema therapy, or a related approach, can hold what you bring in a way a book cannot. The Note at the start of this book pointed in the same direction. I am repeating it here because it matters more in this chapter than almost anywhere else.

If you are managing fine, keep reading. If you are not, please reach out. There is no failure in needing more than a book.

In a Nutshell

The defectiveness belief was learned, often early, from the steady weather of unmet needs. A child concluded, reasonably given the data, that hiding was the safest move. That child was not weak. That child was paying attention. Understanding the origin is not about blame. It is about seeing the belief clearly enough to know that it isn't the truth about you. It is a conclusion drawn by a smaller you who was doing their best. The next chapter is about the parts of yourself that still carry the work that child did, and how to begin to know them, one at a time, with the kindness they have always deserved. You have done enough for this chapter. Close the book if you need to. The rest will be here when you are ready to come back to it.

Chapter 5 The Critic Inside

Eloise sits down at her desk after a 10am meeting and opens a spreadsheet she doesn't need to look at. She is not really looking at the spreadsheet. She is replaying the meeting.

Twenty minutes ago, she said a thing. The thing was small, and was, on reflection, fine. She'd offered a small disagreement with a colleague's timeline. The colleague had nodded. The conversation had moved on. The meeting had ended. Two people had said *thanks, Eloise* on the way out.

The voice in her head is not letting her sit with the *thanks, Eloise*. The voice is replaying the small disagreement, examining her phrasing, pulling out three words she could have chosen better, narrating the way her voice sounded slightly off in the second sentence, wondering if the colleague was actually nodding because she agreed or nodding to make the awkward thing stop sooner. The voice has been doing this for twenty minutes. The voice is, in fact, very good at this. The voice has been doing this for as long as Eloise can remember.

If she had to describe the voice, she'd say it sounded like her own. The voice uses her vocabulary, her sentence rhythms, her judgments of other people. The voice could pass for her on a cursory listen. It's also, somehow, not on her side. It doesn't, when she's honest about it, treat her the way she would treat a friend in the same situation. It treats her the way someone with limited patience would treat a person they had given up expecting much from.

That voice has a name in schema therapy. The technical name is the *punitive parent mode*. I'll use that term once, here, because you might bump into it elsewhere, and then I will mostly call it what it really is. The inner critic. The voice that sounds like you but isn't quite you. The voice that learned its lines from somewhere else.

If you've ever sat at a desk after a small ordinary moment, listening to a voice in your head pull it apart, this chapter is for you.

Here is the principle. The inner critic uses your voice. It does not, in any meaningful sense, write its lines. The lines were written long ago, by someone else, in conditions that no longer apply. You are not arguing with yourself when you argue with it. You are arguing with a recording. The way out is not to win the argument. It is to recognize the recording for what it is, and learn to answer it with a kinder voice that is also yours.

The Critic Uses Your Voice

This is the part most readers find the most useful to understand, so I want to be very clear about it.

The inner critic feels like you. It speaks in your voice. It uses your phrasing. It seems to know everything about you, because it has been listening to your life from the inside for as long as you can remember. When it speaks, it sounds like your own settled, sober assessment of yourself.

It isn't. What you are listening to is a voice you absorbed.

Children learn the voices that are spoken to them. They take in the tone, the vocabulary, the timing, the punishments and the praise. By the time those children are six or seven, the voices have been heard enough times that they no longer need to be spoken aloud by anyone outside. The child can produce them inwardly, in the original voice or in a version of their own. The voices have moved in. They have become part of the inner furniture.

Most of the inner furniture is fine. The voice that tells you to look both ways before crossing the road came from someone, originally, and you don't mind that it lives in you now. It's useful.

The inner critic is also inherited furniture, but it isn't useful in the same way. It tends to be made of the harshest assessments you ever absorbed about yourself, often spoken or implied by people who at the time had power over how you saw yourself. It might have been a parent who handled frustration by criticism. It might have been a teacher who used contempt to motivate. It might have been a sibling who teased you in a way the adults let pass. It might have been the steady atmosphere of a household in which you were measured against a standard you couldn't meet. The original sources vary. The mechanism is the same. You took in the voice, and the voice stayed.

When Eloise is at her desk replaying her sentence, she is not listening to herself. She is listening to a voice that learned its lines from a father who was rarely satisfied. The voice has, over the decades, acquired her vocabulary and her phrasing. The content is still her father's.

Where the Critic Shows Up

The inner critic doesn't show up evenly across the day. It picks its moments. Once you can see the pattern of when it speaks, you have one of the more useful pieces of information this chapter can give you.

It shows up before a social event. Walking to the gathering, you might hear a steady stream of small judgments. *Don't talk too much. Don't be the first one to leave. Don't bring up the thing you were going to bring up. They're going to think you're trying too hard.*

It shows up after a small visible thing. You spoke at a meeting and the voice is, like Eloise's, replaying your phrasing. You sent the message and the voice is mocking the way you signed off. You laughed at a joke that wasn't really funny and the voice is telling you the laughter sounded forced.

It shows up in response to kindness. Someone says something warm to you and the voice, almost instantly, reinterprets it. *They're just being polite. They don't really mean that. They want something. They're saying that to everyone.* The cooling of compliments we talked about in Chapter 3 is, often, the inner critic at work. The defectiveness belief speaks. The critic delivers the line.

Martin, a man in his thirties, told me once that the moment he first really heard his critic was after a friend had texted to say *I'm always glad when I see your name come up*. The text arrived. Martin felt a small warmth. Within fifteen seconds, an internal voice had produced four reasons the friend probably hadn't meant it. By the time Martin replied, he had typed and deleted three versions of his answer trying to find one that wouldn't sound like he was taking the warmth too seriously. The warmth had been small and the response to it had taken thirty minutes. The critic had done its work invisibly, between the warmth arriving and the reply being sent.

It shows up in the small ordinary moments. You walked past your reflection and the voice noted three things. You finished a piece of work and the voice told you it was fine but not very good. You enjoyed yourself for an evening and the voice arrived in the morning to ask whether you really should have.

The pattern varies by person. Some readers find their critic most active in the first hour after a social interaction. Others find it loudest before they sleep. Many find it lives along their commute.

Notice when yours speaks. Notice where it lives. The seeing is the work.

For many readers, the worst hour of the critic is the half-hour before sleep. The lights are out. The day's small visible things are over. There is nothing to do but listen. The voice arrives and runs a slow, thorough audit of the day. The conversation that was a little off. The email that was a little wrong. The thing you almost said and didn't. The thing you said and shouldn't have. The voice doesn't tire the way you do; the voice gets sharper as the room gets darker. Many readers fall asleep eventually with the audit still running. They wake up tired in a way that has nothing to do with how long they slept.

If that is the version of the critic you carry, the audit is what you're trying to interrupt. The naming work this chapter is pointing toward isn't a silencing technique. It is a small wedge under a door that has been closed too long. Even a small wedge changes the room.

Why Arguing Doesn't Work

Here is a thing that most readers have already tried, and that almost never works.

The first response many people have, when they recognize the inner critic, is to argue with it. To answer its statements with counter-statements. *You said that fine. They liked you. The compliment was real. Stop being so harsh.* The arguments feel sensible. They are, on the merits, often right.

The critic is unmoved. Within five minutes it is talking again, sometimes in a slightly louder voice, sometimes with a fresh angle that hadn't occurred to you, sometimes with a quiet sneer at the very fact that you tried to argue. You end the exchange feeling not just criticized but criticized for the attempt to defend yourself.

The reason arguing doesn't work is that the critic isn't a thought. It's an absorbed voice with its own emotional logic. Arguing with it on the level of evidence is like arguing with the weather. The weather doesn't update on the basis of your reasons. It has its own causes. So does the critic.

What works better is not argument but recognition. Naming the voice for what it is. Stepping a small distance back from it, so that you are listening to the recording rather than being inside it. From that distance, a kinder voice can answer, not by arguing with the critic but by speaking past it, the way a friend in the room with you might speak gently to you while a bad noise continued in the background.

Naming Your Critic

Here is the first action of this chapter.

This week, when you next catch your critic in full flow, try doing one thing. Name it.

You can give it a literal name. Some readers find this helpful. They call the voice *the inspector*, or *the headmistress*, or whatever fits. Naming the voice gives it a small character of its own, which puts a little distance between you and it.

You can also just name what it is, without giving it a label. *Oh. That's the critic.* The naming makes the voice an object rather than the air you breathe. An object is something you can look at.

Marcel, the man we met in Chapter 1, told me once that the day he started calling his critic *the foreman* was the first day the voice lost some of its grip. *The foreman thinks I shouldn't have said that*. The sentence sounded different in his head than *I shouldn't have said that*. It put the judgment outside him. He could hear the foreman without being inside the foreman.

You don't have to do this with elaborate ceremony. The first time, in real life, will probably be in the middle of a small mental moment. You will be walking home from somewhere, the voice will be telling you about your evening, and you will say, internally, *that's the critic*. And the voice will keep talking, because the voice does, and you will keep walking. But something will have shifted, just a fraction. You will have heard the voice from outside it, for a second. That's the start.

A First Kinder Sentence

The second action is smaller, and harder, and more important.

Once you have named the critic, write down what a kinder voice would say in the same situation.

You don't have to believe the kinder sentence yet. You don't have to feel it. You only have to write it down. The point is that the sentence exists, in words, on a page, in your own handwriting, as a real alternative to the voice you have been listening to.

A worked example. Eloise's critic, twenty minutes after the meeting, said something like *you sounded ridiculous, three words were wrong, the colleague was nodding to shut you up, everyone in the room noticed.* The kinder sentence Eloise wrote down later that week, in the notebook she had started keeping, said: *I disagreed clearly in a meeting. People said thanks. The phrasing was fine. The colleague nodded because they agreed.*

The kinder sentence isn't a pep talk. It isn't *you're amazing, you nailed it, everyone loved you.* That kind of sentence wouldn't land. Eloise wouldn't believe it. The critic would dismiss it.

The kinder sentence is the sober, accurate, friend-sized version of what actually happened. It is what you would say to a colleague who had told you about the same meeting. It is the sentence the inner critic is not allowing into the room.

Write it down. Keep the page. The kinder voice has to be allowed in at the same pace the critic was kept out. Over weeks of writing these sentences, something starts to shift. The kinder voice isn't louder yet. But it exists. And existence is, eventually, enough.

Catching It Once

Your action this week is small.

Catch your inner critic once. Just once. When you catch it, do two things. Name it. Then write down what a kinder voice would say about the same moment.

Don't try to silence the critic. Don't try to override it. Don't try to do this every time it speaks; the critic speaks often, and you'd be exhausted. Just once. One catching, one naming, one kinder sentence on a page.

What you are doing, when you do this, is teaching a different voice to exist. The new voice doesn't replace the old one. The old one will go on speaking, often loudly. The new voice just earns a place in the room. Over time, the new voice gets a little louder. The old voice gets a little softer. The shift is slow. It is also real.

A small note on patience. The voice that has been criticizing you was, in some readers, the loudest voice in your inner life for thirty years. It will not be displaced by one kinder sentence on a Tuesday afternoon. The work is the practice of returning to the kinder sentence, week after week, until the kinder voice begins to feel like one of your voices too.

In a Nutshell

The inner critic uses your voice but didn't write its lines. The lines were absorbed, long ago, from people whose voices became your inner furniture. Arguing with the critic doesn't work. The critic isn't a thought; it's a recording. What works is naming it, stepping back from it, and allowing a kinder voice, written down in sober accurate sentences, to begin to exist alongside it. Catch the critic once this week. Name it. Write the kinder sentence on a page. Keep the page. The kinder voice has to be allowed in at the same pace the critic was kept out.

Chapter 6 The Wall That Protects You

Ines is at her partner's parents' house for Sunday lunch. She's on her third visit. The first two had been fine. This one is going slightly wrong in the way Sunday lunches sometimes go slightly wrong, which is to say not catastrophically, just enough to require attention.

Her partner's mother has said something about Ines's work that landed in a place neither of them intended. Ines, in real time, knows that the mother didn't mean it the way it sounded. The mother knows the mother didn't mean it the way it sounded. The whole table knows it was a small bump that needed to be smoothed over with a kind sentence and a slight change of subject.

Ines watches herself, from a small distance, stop being able to access the kind sentence.

She doesn't, in the moment, choose this. She doesn't decide to go quiet. What happens is that the lively, conversational part of her that had been carrying the lunch goes off somewhere, the way a radio loses a signal in a tunnel. What's left at the table is a polite, smaller, more careful version of her that can pass for the original on a quick glance.

She finishes the lunch. She thanks her partner's parents. She walks to the car. She says, when her partner asks how it was, that it was nice. By the time they're back at the flat she has remembered three things she could have said in the moment and didn't.

What happened, between the small bump and the smaller Ines who finished the meal, has a name. Schema therapists call this *the detached protector mode*. I'll use that term once, here, and then mostly call it what it is. The wall. The bodyguard. The thing that goes up, often without your permission, when the situation seems to be asking more of you than the part of you in charge of self-protection thinks is safe.

If you've ever watched yourself check out in real time and could not, in the moment, stop it, this chapter is for you.

Here is the principle. The wall isn't a flaw. It isn't a failure of nerve. It is a strategy you learned, possibly very young, that has been keeping you from a particular kind of pain for a long time. It is doing exactly what it was built to do. The work of this chapter isn't to demolish the wall. The work is to recognize it going up, name it gently, and start to understand what it has been trying to protect.

The Wall Did Its Job

The wall, like the critic, is a thing you learned. Unlike the critic, the wall is mostly a behavior rather than a voice. It is the going quiet, the going numb, the disappearing, the giving short answers, the watching yourself from a small distance, the leaving early in your head before you've left in your body.

It got built somewhere. For some readers, the wall was built around a childhood in which staying fully present was unsafe, and going somewhere else, internally, was the only available exit. For others, it was built around moments in which being known had cost too much and the wall arrived to make sure those moments didn't happen again. For most, it was a slow accumulation. Small situations in which being more present hadn't gone well. The wall got a little thicker each time.

The wall is not, in any moral sense, a problem. It is an old strategy that worked. The eight-year-old who learned to go somewhere else mentally when the adults were arguing was, in that moment, a small genius. The teenager who learned to give short answers at the family dinner instead of opening up was protecting something they didn't yet have the words for. The young adult who learned to leave early in their head, while their body finished the conversation, was managing what they had to manage.

If you carry the wall in your adult life, you do so because it has been useful. The trouble isn't that it exists. The trouble is that it has stayed useful long after the original situations stopped being there. It rises in present-day rooms that don't require it. It rises during Sunday lunches that don't, by any sober assessment, need a bodyguard. The strategy hasn't updated. Strategies, unhelped, rarely do.

What the Wall Looks Like in You

The wall is easier to spot when you know what it looks like from the inside.

For some readers, it looks like going quiet. The conversation continues, but you are no longer in it the way you were a minute ago. Your contributions become shorter, more polite, more on the surface. The room would not necessarily notice the shift. You can feel it.

For others, it looks like going numb. Something happens, sometimes something kind, sometimes something difficult, and the feeling you'd have expected to have doesn't quite arrive. There is a slight flatness where the feeling should be. You can name what is happening but you can't quite feel it. Hugo, the man at the birthday party from Chapter 2, described this once as being in the room with a panel of glass between him and the room.

For others, it looks like disappearing. You are still physically there, but a part of you has gone elsewhere. Some readers say they go into their own heads. Others say they go behind their eyes. Others describe an almost watching-from-outside sense, observing themselves talk to other people while feeling the talking from a small distance.

For others, it looks like the screen. The phone comes out. The wall is sometimes built of small everyday avoidances of the present, and the screen is the wall's most modern brick. The friend asks the deeper question; the phone vibrates; the moment passes.

For others again, the wall is loudest in conflict. Mateo, the man we met in the Introduction, told me once about the moment his partner first asked him a hard question about their relationship, a question the partner had been working up to for weeks. Mateo could feel, in real time, that this was a moment that needed him present. He could also feel, in real time, the wall going up faster than he could think. By the time he answered, his voice was flat, his answers were short, and the words he was producing were technically responsive without being in any way truthful. The wall had taken the conversation away from him before he'd been able to stay in it. He didn't tell his partner this for another six months.

These are different versions of the same thing. They are the wall doing what walls do. They are not, in any of these versions, character flaws. They are old protections, still on duty.

The Early Signs

Here is the most useful skill this chapter can give you. Most walls have early signs, before they are fully up. If you can spot the early signs, you have a small window in which other moves become possible.

The early signs vary by person. They might include a small physical thing. A tightening in the chest. A faint pulling-back of the breath. A subtle sense of your face going neutral. They might include a thought pattern. A sudden mental rehearsal of the exit. A scanning of the room for who is least demanding. A quiet calculation of how soon the conversation might end. They might include an emotional flatness. The feeling you had a minute ago has gone slightly quieter. You can still talk. You just don't feel quite there.

The signs are usually small. You have been ignoring them for years, because they have been part of the steady weather of your life. The work is to start noticing them, gently, without trying to do anything with them yet.

Julian, the man whose family example we met in Chapter 1, started noticing that the wall came up for him at a specific physical cue. His shoulders would lift, just slightly. He had carried the lifted shoulders for years without realizing they were a signal. Once he noticed, he could feel the wall starting to rise before it had fully reached him.

You don't have to find a body cue. The signs can be anywhere. The point is just to start watching.

What the Wall Costs

A piece of this that often gets missed.

The wall protects you from a specific kind of pain. It protects you from the moment in which you might be seen and found wanting. It protects you from saying the thing that could be misunderstood, asking for something that could be refused, opening into a conversation that could turn sharp. It has been doing this protective work, in some readers' lives, for thirty or forty years. Across that span, the wall has saved you from a great deal of small daily wounding. Take a moment to acknowledge that. It has been keeping you safe, in its way, for a long time.

It has also cost you. This is the part the wall doesn't show you, because the wall isn't built to show you costs. The wall is built to keep you in the safe place. The cost lives in everything that the safe place excludes.

The cost is the closeness that never quite arrived. The relationships that stayed at a certain distance. The opportunities you didn't quite step toward. The conversations you didn't quite have. The version of you that didn't quite come out, because coming out felt like more than you could risk that day. Each individual cost is small. The accumulation, across decades, is large.

Naming the cost isn't about blaming the wall. It's about beginning to want something it can't give you. The wall was built to keep you safe. It wasn't built to give you a full life. Those are not the same thing, and a quiet part of you has known that for a while.

Why You Can't Talk Your Way Past It

A pattern you may have already noticed.

Once the wall is up, telling yourself to be more present rarely works. The reminder lands, the part of you that hears it agrees, and the wall stays exactly where it is. You can sit through a whole evening lecturing yourself internally about being more engaged. You will not be more engaged. The wall is not in the part of you that hears lectures.

This is the same lesson as the critic. The protective patterns, once they are running, don't yield to argument. They yield to recognition. They yield to being seen for what they are, named for what they are, and given a little room to soften on their own.

What you are aiming for, in the long run, is the wall feeling, gradually, that the present-day rooms don't require it. The wall doesn't soften because you've ordered it to. It softens because the conditions have changed.

The conditions change in two ways. The first is that the rooms you live in genuinely become safer, sometimes because you've chosen different rooms, sometimes because the rooms you already had have shifted with time. The second is that the part of you that built the wall begins, over months, to trust that you, the adult, are now able to handle the rooms that used to require its full protection. Both kinds of change matter. Neither is fast. The wall does not soften on a deadline. It softens in its own time, when it stops being needed in the way it used to be.

This is also why progress on the wall can feel oddly invisible. The wall doesn't announce its softening. You will notice, after some months, that a particular kind of conversation has been easier than it used to be, or that a particular kind of gathering ended without you having checked out. Those moments are the softening. They look like nothing. They are something.

Naming It as It Rises

The first action this chapter asks for is small.

This week, when you notice the wall rising, name it. Internally, in plain words. *Oh. The wall is going up.*

Don't try to push it down. Don't try to override it. Don't promise yourself you'll be more present at the next gathering. Just name it.

The naming does something quiet but real. It moves the wall from being the air you are breathing to being a thing you have noticed. A thing that has been noticed is no longer in full charge of you. A thing that has been noticed is, by a small margin, something you can be with rather than inside.

A Small Grounding Pause

A small technique for when the wall is rising and you want to give yourself a quiet alternative.

Notice five things around you that you can see. Not in a special way, just literally five things. The lamp. The corner of the table. A book on a shelf. The texture of someone's sweater. A water glass.

Notice three things you can hear. The hum of the fridge. Someone talking. A car outside.

Notice one thing you can feel. The chair under you. The floor. The temperature of your hands.

This is a standard sensory grounding practice, drawn from work with trauma and dissociation that found small acts of attention to the present can interrupt the slide toward checking out (Najavits, 2002). It does not require concentration. It requires only one minute of attention to the room you are in. The wall has been pulling you out of the room. The grounding gently puts you back, without forcing anything.

You can do this in the middle of a Sunday lunch with no one knowing. You can do it walking back to your desk. You can do it standing at the kitchen sink. It doesn't always work; nothing always works. It is something to have in your pocket.

One Noticing This Week

Your action this week is just one. Notice the wall rising once. Name it to yourself in plain words. If you want to, do the small grounding pause. That's the entire assignment.

Don't try to do this every time the wall rises this week. You'll exhaust yourself and the practice will become another job. Just once, with care.

What you are doing, when you notice the wall this way, is starting a quiet conversation with the part of you that built it. You are letting that part know you have seen what it does. You are not trying to fire it from its job. You are just letting it know you are aware. Awareness, slowly, is what allows old patterns to soften.

In a Nutshell

The wall, the going quiet, the going numb, the disappearing, was a strategy you learned and that worked. It still works, in its old way, in present-day situations that don't require it. The work isn't to demolish the wall. The work is to notice it rising, name it for what it is, and let the noticing be its own slow signal that the old protection is no longer needed everywhere it shows up. Name it once this week. Use the grounding pause if it helps. The naming is the start of the softening.

Chapter 7 The Younger You

Before we start, a note to read first.

This chapter touches material that for some readers will be light and for others will be heavier. The exercises below are deliberately small and contained. They are not designed to take you anywhere difficult. If you start them and the heaviness rises past what you can hold by yourself, please put the book down and consider whether the work this chapter is pointing toward is work you would be better doing with a therapist beside you. Some of the most important parts of this material are genuinely done better in company. There is no failure in pausing here.

That said, here is what the chapter offers, if you are ready.

Coralie is at a hairdresser's appointment. She's been to this hairdresser before. She likes him. The salon is quiet. He shows her a photograph on his phone of a haircut he is suggesting for her. The haircut is nice. She likes the haircut. She is about to say so.

What comes out of her mouth instead is a slightly uncertain *whatever you think.*

She walks home an hour later with a haircut that is fine, that she'll get used to, that isn't what she would have chosen. She isn't really thinking about the haircut. She's thinking about the small thing that happened in the chair, in the half-second before she said the wrong sentence. For a moment, in front of the photograph, she had felt very small. She had felt, briefly and without explanation, six years old.

The six was specific. It wasn't a metaphor she invented later. In the moment, in the chair, the part of her that took over the answer wasn't her adult self. It was someone she had once been, who hadn't been allowed to choose haircuts.

If you've ever had a moment like Coralie's, the moment in which something small in the present pulled something old in close enough to take the wheel for a second, this chapter is for you. It is also the chapter I want you to read most slowly.

Here is the principle. The younger you, the part that learned to hide, isn't a metaphor. It is the version of you that did the original work of survival, and it is still in there, still small, still bracing. The work of this chapter isn't to send you back into anything difficult. It's to introduce, in a small and bounded way, the steadier adult you are now to the part of you that has been waiting. You don't have to relive what that younger you lived through. You only have to begin to offer them the kindness no one had time to offer them then.

The Part That Is Still There

Schema therapy gives the younger part of you a name. The technical name is the *lonely child mode* or *abandoned child mode*, depending on the texture of the experience it carries. I'll use those terms once, because some readers will encounter them elsewhere, and then I will mostly call it the younger you.

The younger you isn't a metaphor for general inner sensitivity. It is, in clinical descriptions and in the felt experience of many readers, a specific part of self that holds the original belief, the original feelings, and the original sense of having to manage something larger than they should have had to manage (Young et al., 2003).

The younger you doesn't usually take the wheel of your adult life. Most of the time, the adult you who is doing the reading is in charge. But there are moments, often small and benign-looking from the outside, in which the younger you comes close enough to influence the answer.

Coralie at the hairdresser is one of those moments. The hairdresser hadn't done anything wrong. The salon was safe. The haircut wasn't important. But the photograph, for whatever reason, had been close enough to a younger memory of being told what she would wear that the younger Coralie had stirred. The adult Coralie had answered with the younger Coralie's words.

You may not remember a specific moment like that one. You may, alternatively, remember many. Either way, the part of you that holds the old feelings is in there. The work of this chapter is to begin, in a small way, to know that part of you.

Why It Still Matters

Some readers, at this point, wonder why it matters. The younger you is decades ago. The original conditions are gone. Why would the work of an adult life involve any attention to that part of self at all?

The answer is in the moments. The defectiveness belief we named in Chapter 3 isn't held by the adult mind. The adult mind can see, on a sober afternoon, that the belief isn't quite true. The belief is held in the younger part of you that originally formed it. It is held in the same place where the original feelings are still held. As long as that part of you is sealed off from the adult kindness you would otherwise be able to offer them, the belief stays put.

This is why purely cognitive work may not be enough for some early, emotionally held beliefs. In schema therapy and imagery rescripting, change often involves contacting the felt memory or younger part that has been carrying the belief, not only debating the belief from the adult mind (Arntz & Weertman, 1999; Young et al., 2003).

That contact, done badly, can be retraumatizing. That contact, done well and in small bounded ways, can be one of the more useful things a person ever learns. This chapter is one careful version of doing it small.

Many Readers Find

Many readers, the first time they sit with the idea of a younger version of themselves, find one of a few things.

Some find resistance. The whole framing feels strange. They can't quite imagine the younger them as a real part of self. That is fine. The exercises below are written so that they work whether you can vividly picture the younger you or only sense them faintly.

Some find a quiet sadness rising. The idea that there is a small version of themselves still in there, still carrying what they carried, lands with a small heaviness. The heaviness is appropriate. It is the beginning of the grief and the kindness this chapter is pointing toward. Let it be what it is. Don't push it away.

Some find that the resistance and the sadness alternate. They sit with the idea for a few minutes; the resistance arrives, then a glimpse of the younger self, then the resistance again. This is also fine. The contact doesn't have to be deep. It has to be small.

Some find, especially if their early experiences were difficult, that even the idea of the younger self brings up more than they can hold without help. If that is your experience right now, please consider closing the chapter and reading it later, possibly with a therapist beside you. This work isn't supposed to overwhelm you.

What They Needed

You don't have to know what the younger you went through, in detail, to know what they needed.

The needs of a child, in general, are simple to name and difficult to provide. They needed to feel safe with the adults around them.

They needed to feel that their feelings were taken seriously rather than corrected, named for them, or dismissed. They needed to be liked for what they were, rather than for what they performed. They needed to be allowed to make small mistakes without becoming a problem. They needed to be allowed to be a child.

In schema therapy language these are called core childhood needs. Different writers list them slightly differently. The point isn't the list. The point is that for many readers of this book, one or several of those needs went unmet often enough to teach the defectiveness belief.

The younger you was missing something. What they were missing was simple. They needed someone to stay.

The adult you can, in small ways, begin to be that someone. Not by going back into what happened. By offering, inwardly, in safety, in the present, what the younger you didn't get.

A Small Letter

Here is the first exercise, and the one to do most carefully.

Find a quiet half hour when you won't be interrupted. Sit somewhere comfortable. Have a piece of paper, or open a blank document.

Picture the youngest version of yourself you can clearly recall in a neutral moment. Not a moment of distress. A moment of doing something they liked, or sitting somewhere they often sat, or being themselves in a setting that wasn't going wrong. If you can't picture a specific moment, picture a school photograph or any image of yourself at that age that you've seen.

Then write a short letter to that younger you.

The letter doesn't have to do anything ambitious. It can be very short. Three or four sentences is plenty. Tell them, in your adult voice, what you'd want them to know now. Not advice. Not reassurance you don't believe. Just the kind, sober, accurate version of what an adult who cared about them might have said.

You were doing your best with what you had.

The things you were carrying weren't yours to carry.

You weren't too much. You weren't too sensitive. You were exactly right.

I can see how hard you were working not to take up space.

I'm here now. I'm sorry it took so long.

You don't have to use any of those sentences. They are examples. Use what comes up in your own words.

Some readers, doing this for the first time, will find tears arriving without warning. Some will find a tightness in the chest. Some will find nothing in particular, just the writing. All of those are fine. None of them are wrong.

When you've written the letter, fold it, or close the document, and set it aside. Don't immediately do anything else with it. Sit for a minute. The work is in the writing. The sitting afterward is its own piece.

Felix, the man whose childhood we touched on in Chapter 4, told me later about the first letter he wrote to his eight-year-old self. He hadn't been able to picture the eight-year-old at first. He'd had to find an actual photograph from a family album. He looked at the photograph for a long time before he could write anything. The letter, when it came, was four sentences long. *I see how hard you were trying not to be any trouble. You weren't any trouble. The quiet wasn't because you were broken; it was because you were being kind to people who were tired. You can stop now.* He cried, in a way that surprised him, while writing the third sentence. He sat with the letter for a few minutes. He put it in a drawer.

Two months later, he told me, he noticed that the eight-year-old felt, for the first time he could remember, slightly less alone. He had not done anything ambitious. He had written four sentences. The relationship had started.

A Grounding Pause for If It Gets Too Much

Some readers will not need this. Some will. Have it in your pocket either way.

If, at any point in the exercise, the feeling rises past what you can comfortably hold, stop. Look around the room you're actually in. Name five things you can see. Three you can hear. One you can feel. The same grounding pause we used in the last chapter. Bring your attention back to the adult you, in this room, with this body, in this moment.

You don't have to finish the letter today. You don't have to finish the chapter today. There is no test at the end. The younger you has waited a long time. They can wait until you're ready.

Three Kind Sentences

Your action this week is small.

Pick three kind sentences to say, inwardly, to the younger you. They can be from the list above or in your own words. Choose ones you can imagine being able to say without it feeling false.

Once during the week, when you have a quiet minute, say the three sentences to the younger you inwardly. Once is enough. You can do it walking somewhere, lying in bed, sitting in the car before going into a meeting. Three sentences. Said with care.

You may feel something. You may feel nothing. You may feel something the next day, or the week after. The work doesn't depend on the immediate feeling. It depends on the steady, slow building of an inner relationship that wasn't there before.

If you've spent decades not knowing this part of yourself was in there, the first contact will feel small. It is supposed to. The younger you doesn't need a grand speech. They need someone to notice they exist, and to come back to them, briefly and kindly, more than once. That is the whole practice.

This is the relationship that, over time, makes everything else in the book possible. The chapters ahead are about building a life that the younger you, the inner critic, and the wall can all begin to trust. The work begins here.

When to Pause and Get Support

Closing this chapter with the same note it opened with.

If the material here brought up more than the chapter has helped you hold, please consider reaching out for professional support. A therapist who knows schema therapy, or a related approach, can work alongside you on the parts of this that books can't reach. The Note at the beginning of the book pointed in this direction. I am pointing again.

Self-help and therapy are not opposites. The reading you have done so far is not lessened by deciding that the next steps are better taken in company. Some of the most important things a person can work on are genuinely done better with a witness who can hold what arises. If this chapter has shown you that you might be ready for that, that is itself a piece of progress.

In a Nutshell

The younger you, the part that learned to hide, is still in there. They have been waiting. The work of this chapter isn't to go back into what they went through. It's to begin, in a small and contained way, to offer them what they needed. A short letter. Three kind sentences. A grounding pause if it gets too much. The relationship being built here is the relationship that makes the rest of the book possible. Go slowly. If you need help, ask for it. The younger you has waited this long. There is no rush, and there will not be a test. The next chapter takes the work outward, into how the pattern shows up in the relationships you have today.

Chapter 8 Close but Not Too Close

Lucia has been seeing someone for six months, and it is going well, which is the problem.

She wouldn't have put it that way out loud. If a friend asked, she'd say things were good, and mean it. He is kind. He is funny in the specific way she likes. He remembers things she said weeks ago. The relationship has the quality, rare in her experience, of being easy.

Last Tuesday he left a toothbrush at her flat. He didn't make a thing of it. He just, on his way out, asked if it was okay to leave it so he didn't have to keep bringing one. She said of course. She meant it, in the moment.

By Thursday she had begun, without quite deciding to, building a case against him.

The case was subtle. It was made of small observations she had not made before the toothbrush. The way he laughed slightly too loud at his own jokes. A political opinion of his that she had previously found endearing and now found slightly grating. A sense, hard to pin down, that they might not want the same things in the long run. None of the observations was large. Together they formed a quiet, accumulating argument that this relationship, the good one, the easy one, might not be right after all.

Lucia has done this four times before. She has, in fact, a track record. Each of her previous relationships ended at roughly the point this one has reached, the point where it stopped being a beginning and started being a thing with a future. Each time, she experienced the ending as a sober recognition that the person wasn't, on closer inspection, right for her. Each time, she was the one who left. Each time, she was sure she was being honest.

She isn't, in any of these cases, a villain. She isn't playing games. She genuinely feels the doubts when they arrive, and the doubts genuinely feel like wisdom. What she hasn't been able to see, from inside the pattern, is that the doubts arrive on a schedule. They arrive when the relationship gets close enough to matter. They are not, mostly, about the man. They are about what the closeness has started to risk.

If you've ever found yourself building a quiet case against someone right at the point things got good, this chapter is for you.

Here is the principle. The fear of being rejected doesn't keep you safe from rejection. It arranges for a smaller, earlier, self-administered version of it. You leave before you can be left. You pull back to see if they pull back too, and the pulling back makes them pull back, and you take their response as proof. The push and the pull are not two different things. They are the same fear, wearing two faces.

The Push and the Pull

Most readers with this pattern feel both a push and a pull, often about the same person, sometimes in the same hour.

The pull is the longing. It's the part of you that wants to be known, wants to be close, wants the toothbrush in the bathroom and the standing Sunday plans and the person who remembers what you said weeks ago. The pull is real. It's not a weakness, and it's not something to be ashamed of. It's the most human thing about you.

The push is the fear. It's the part of you that, the moment the pull starts to be answered, begins to manage the risk. Closeness means you could be left. Being known means you could be found wanting. The push arrives to make sure that, if the bad thing is going to happen, it happens on your terms, early, before you've invested too much, before the loss could be too big.

The trouble is that the push and the pull point in opposite directions, and you feel both. So you get close, then you retreat. You answer the warm message, then you go quiet for three days. You let someone in, then you find the reasons they shouldn't have been let in. From the outside, this can look like mixed signals, or like not knowing what you want. From the inside, it's perfectly coherent. You want the closeness, and you are terrified of it, and both are true at once.

The defectiveness belief we named in Chapter 3 is the engine underneath. If you believe, somewhere deep, that you are not, in the end, enough, then closeness isn't safe. Closeness is the thing that will eventually reveal the truth. The push is the belief, protecting you from the moment of being seen and found wanting. It would rather you lose the relationship now, on purpose, than lose it later, by exposure.

Leaving Before You're Left

The cleanest version of the push is the preemptive exit. You leave first.

Leaving first feels, from the inside, like strength. It feels like clarity. It feels like you saw something the other person didn't, and acted on it before you got hurt. There's a grim satisfaction in being the one who ended it. You were not, this time, the one left behind.

What leaving first actually does is guarantee the loss while letting you avoid the part you fear most, which isn't the loss itself but the experience of being the one who is rejected. By leaving first, you trade a possible rejection later for a certain ending now, and you call the trade wisdom.

Lucia's four previous relationships all ended this way. In each, she experienced herself as the discerning one who'd spotted the flaw. In each, the man was, by her later admission, bewildered, because things had been going well. She had not lied to them or to herself. She had simply felt the doubts arrive, on schedule, right when the closeness reached the threshold, and she had trusted the doubts because the doubts felt like her own clear judgment.

Reviews of this pattern describe withdrawal, fear of rejection, and impairment across social and intimate relationships; clinically, that withdrawal can help produce the isolation the person most fears (Lampe & Malhi, 2018). The fear writes the outcome. The thing you did to stay safe is the thing that costs you the closeness.

The Test That Rigs Itself

A subtler version of the push is the test.

The test works like this. Some part of you, not fully conscious, wants to know whether the other person will leave. So you pull back, slightly, to see what they do. You go a little quiet. You become a little less available. You wait to see whether they come find you.

Here is the trouble with the test. The other person can't see the test. They can only see the pulling-back. So when you go quiet, they often, reasonably, give you space. They read your withdrawal as a signal that you want distance, and they provide it. You then experience their space-giving as proof. *See. They didn't come find me. They didn't really care.*

The test rigs itself. You set up a situation that can only confirm the fear, and then you collect the confirmation. The other person, meanwhile, has no idea they were being tested, and no idea they failed.

Coralie, whose hairdresser moment we met in Chapter 7, ran this test for years on a close friend. She would withdraw slightly when she felt the friendship getting important, wait to see if the friend chased, and feel quietly wounded when the friend, respecting the apparent need for space, didn't. The friend had no idea. From the friend's side, Coralie simply went quiet sometimes, and the kind thing seemed to be to let her have her quiet. Two people who cared about each other, both behaving reasonably, both ending up further apart.

Friendship Does It Too

The push and the pull aren't only about romance. They run through friendships just as reliably.

Mateo, who we met in the Introduction, has known Felix since they were eight. They text twice a year. Mateo composes longer messages to Felix in his head than he ever sends. Every few months he thinks about suggesting they meet. The thought arrives with a small warmth, the pull, and is followed almost immediately by a small set of reasons not to, the push. Felix is probably busy. It's been too long; it would be awkward to reach out now. Felix would come if Mateo asked, but Mateo can't quite be sure of that, and the not-being-sure is enough to stop him.

So the friendship, which both men value, sits at twice-a-year, held there by a push that Felix can't see and Mateo can barely name. Neither of them is doing anything wrong. The friendship is just quietly starved by a fear that lives on only one side of it.

If you have a Felix, someone you'd be closer to if the push didn't keep intercepting the pull, you are not unusual. Most readers of this book have several.

When the Push Wins for Years

The push doesn't only end relationships. Often it does something quieter and more durable. It keeps them at a fixed distance for years, neither ending nor deepening.

Sebastian, whose sister we met in Chapter 1, has a marriage that looks, from the outside, settled and fine. He and his wife are kind to each other. They've been together eleven years. They've also, by Sebastian's private admission, never quite been close in the way he sees other couples be close. He keeps a small distance, so habitual he doesn't experience it as distance. He shares the news of his days and withholds the weather of his inner life. His wife has, over the years, stopped asking for more, because the asking kept meeting the wall. They've arrived at a steady, affectionate, slightly lonely equilibrium that neither of them chose and both maintain.

This is the push winning slowly. Not a dramatic exit. A relationship quietly held at arm's length for a decade, by a fear that one person carries and neither names. Many long marriages and long friendships have this shape. They're not failing. They're just being lived at the half volume we'll talk about in the next chapter, in the one arena where it costs the most.

The reason this matters is that the slow version is easy to miss. The preemptive exit at least announces itself; the relationship ends and you can see the pattern. The slow version hides inside a relationship that's still technically working, which is exactly why it can run for years before anyone notices what it's been costing.

Why the Good Ones Trigger It Most

Here is the part that surprises people. The push tends to fire hardest not in the bad relationships but in the good ones.

This seems backward until you understand the fear underneath. A relationship that isn't going well doesn't threaten much. There's nothing to lose. The push stays quiet. A relationship that's going well, that's becoming real, that you've started to want, is the one with everything to lose. So that's the one the push works hardest to protect you from.

This is why so many readers can look back at a history of relationships that ended right as they got good, and friendships that faded right as they deepened. It wasn't bad luck. It wasn't a string of wrong people. It was the push, firing reliably at the threshold of real closeness, doing the job it was built to do.

The good news, and there's good news, is that the push is a pattern, and patterns can be seen, and what can be seen can begin to change.

Mapping Your Push and Pull

Here is the first action of this chapter.

Take a relationship, current or past, that mattered to you. Draw two columns on a page. Label one *the pull* and one *the push.*

In the pull column, write what drew you toward the person. What you wanted. What was good. What you longed for.

In the push column, write the moves you made to manage the closeness. The going quiet. The case you built. The reasons you found. The exit you took or wanted to take. The test you ran. Be honest. This is for you alone.

Then look at the timing. When did the push fire? What had just happened in the relationship right before it did? For many readers, a clear pattern appears. The push fired right when the closeness crossed a threshold. The toothbrush. The *I love you.* The invitation to meet the family. The moment it became real.

You're not doing this to feel bad. You're doing it to see the pattern from outside, the way we've been practicing since Chapter 1. Seeing the push fire on a schedule is the thing that, over time, lets you catch it before it acts.

A note on what you'll probably find. Most readers, doing this honestly, discover that their push has a signature move. One person's push is the quiet exit. Another's is the manufactured doubt, like Lucia's case against a good man. Another's is the test, the withdrawal that waits to see if it's chased. Another's is simply the slow arm's length, like Sebastian's. Yours will have a shape. Once you know the shape, you can recognize it the next time it starts, which is the whole point of mapping it now.

One Relationship to Tend

Here is the second action, and the one to actually do this week.

Pick one relationship you want to tend. Not the hardest one. Not the most loaded one. A friendship that faded that you'd like back. A connection you've been letting thin. Someone you think about reaching out to and then talk yourself out of.

Now send one small message you'd normally talk yourself out of.

It doesn't have to be a grand reconnection. It can be small. *Thought of you today, hope you're well. Saw this and it reminded me of you. It's been too long, would be good to catch up sometime.* Send it before the push can build its case. The case will start building the moment you think of sending. Send it anyway, while the pull is still warm.

You don't control what comes back. The other person might reply warmly, might reply slowly, might not reply at all. That's not the point. The point is that, for once, you let the pull win, instead of the push. One message. That's the whole assignment.

In a Nutshell

The push and the pull are the same fear wearing two faces. You want closeness, and you're terrified of it, and both are true at once.

The fear of being rejected doesn't keep you safe from rejection; it arranges a smaller, earlier, self-administered version of it. You leave before you're left. You test in ways that rig themselves. And the push fires hardest in the good relationships, because those are the ones with everything to lose. The push is a pattern. Patterns can be seen, and what can be seen can change. This week, pick one relationship to tend, and send one small message before the push can talk you out of it.

Chapter 9 The Life You Hold Back From

Clara has had a job posting open in a browser tab for eleven days.

The posting is, by any sober assessment, written for her. It's a step up from her current role, at a company she respects, doing work she's good at and would like more of. She has read it perhaps thirty times. She has, twice, started the application. She has, twice, closed the tab before finishing.

Clara has worked at her current company for eleven years. She is, by common agreement, the most knowledgeable person on her team. She is also, by her own description, the least visible. Two people hired three years after her now sit a level above her. Her manager has told her, more than once, that she should put herself forward more. Clara nods, agrees, and doesn't.

The job posting will close on Friday. It's Wednesday. Clara knows, with the same quiet certainty she brings to most of these moments, that she won't apply. She'll find a reason. The reason will sound practical. The timing isn't right. The commute is slightly worse. She's not quite ready. The reasons will be sensible enough that she won't have to notice that the real reason is older and simpler. Applying means being seen. Being seen means being judged. The posting will close, and Clara will feel a small, specific flatness, and she'll close the tab, and the eleventh year will become the twelfth.

If you've ever let an opportunity close while you watched, knowing you wanted it and unable to reach for it, this chapter is for you.

Here is the principle. The avoidant pattern doesn't only cost you closeness. It quietly shrinks the whole footprint of your life. The job not applied for. The idea not raised. The talent kept hidden. The opportunity let go. Each refusal is small, and each one is explainable, and together, across years, they produce a life lived at half volume. The cost is paid not in any single dramatic loss but in the slow accumulation of the things you didn't reach for.

A Life at Half Volume

The phrase I want to give you for this is *a life lived at half volume.*

It captures something the more dramatic language misses. People with this pattern rarely crash their lives. They don't, mostly, blow things up. What they do is live carefully, a half-step back from the full version of whatever they're doing. The career is fine, just smaller than it could have been. The friendships are pleasant, just thinner than they might have been. The interests are real, just kept private. Nothing is obviously wrong. The volume is just turned down, on everything, all the time, and has been for so long that the half volume sounds, to the person living it, like the normal volume of a life.

The research backs the cost up plainly. Avoidant personality disorder is associated with significant impairment across work and social functioning (Grant et al., 2004; Lampe & Malhi, 2018). The impairment doesn't usually show up as crisis. It shows up as a quiet, durable underperformance relative to the person's actual capacity. The most prepared person in the room, who is also the least visible. The most capable, who is somehow always a level below where their capability would predict.

That gap, between what you could do and what you let yourself do, is the cost of the pattern in the part of your life that isn't about relationships at all.

There's a particular grief that comes with seeing this gap, and it's worth naming. It's the grief of capability unspent. Many readers with this pattern are, by any external measure, talented. They are often the competent ones, the reliable ones, the ones who could clearly do more. The grief isn't that they lack ability. It's that the ability has been there all along, held back, while less able and less careful people moved past them into the lives those readers could have had. That grief is real, and this chapter isn't going to pretend it away. But grief, looked at clearly, can become information. It can tell you where you've been holding back, which is the first step toward holding back a little less.

The Cost Compounds

Here's the part that makes the half volume so expensive over time. The costs compound.

A single declined opportunity isn't much. But opportunities build on each other. The promotion you didn't take is also the more senior role you're now not in the running for, which is also the network you didn't build, which is also the confidence you didn't accumulate from having done hard things and survived. Each refusal removes not just the thing refused but the staircase it would have led to. Across a decade, the person who reached and the person who held back aren't one step apart. They're a whole flight of stairs apart, and the gap widens every year.

The same is true socially. The connection you didn't deepen this year is the close friend you don't have in five years, which is the support you don't have in ten, which is the loneliness that gets harder to fix the longer it runs. Avoidance isn't a fixed tax. It's compound interest, charged against the life you could have had, and the bill grows quietly in the background whether or not you're looking at it.

I'm not telling you this to frighten you. I'm telling you because the compounding cuts both ways. Small steps toward being seen also compound. The one application sent leads to the role, which leads to the next, which builds the confidence that makes the one after easier. You don't have to overhaul your life. You have to change the direction of the compounding, by a few degrees, starting with something small. The rest of this book is about how.

The Job Not Applied For

Clara's tab is the most common version. The opportunity that's right there, that you want, that you watch yourself decline.

It's worth being precise about what stops her, because it isn't laziness and it isn't lack of ambition. Clara is ambitious. She wants the bigger role. What stops her is that applying is an act of being seen, of saying *I think I'm good enough for this,* and the defectiveness belief cannot let that statement stand. The belief, working quietly, produces the practical reasons. The reasons are the belief's cover story. Clara experiences the cover story as her own sensible judgment, the same way Lucia experienced her doubts about a good relationship as her own clear judgment in the last chapter. The mechanism is identical. Only the arena is different.

The Idea Not Shared

A smaller daily version is the idea not raised.

Eloise, who we met in Chapter 5, has good ideas in meetings and watches other people say them. She has described the specific experience of forming an idea, rehearsing how she'd say it, and then sitting in the small gap before she'd have to speak while the window closes. Someone else says something near it. The room responds. Eloise feels a flat, familiar disappointment and says nothing.

This happens, for some readers, several times a week. Each instance is tiny. None of them would register as a loss if you described your day. But the accumulation, across a career, is the difference between being known as the person with the ideas and being known as the quiet one who's very good at their job. Eloise has the ideas. She just keeps letting other people be the ones who said them.

The Talent Kept Hidden

The version that often hurts most is the talent kept private.

Many readers carry something they're good at and don't let anyone see. They write and don't show anyone. They make music in a spare room. They have a craft, a skill, a creative thing they're quietly excellent at, kept entirely out of view. The hiding isn't because the talent is small. It's often because the talent matters, and anything that matters is too dangerous to expose to judgment.

Noemi, whose social anxiety work we touched on in Chapter 2, had been painting seriously for a decade when she first mentioned it, almost in passing, as though it were nothing. She had never shown the paintings to anyone. Not because they were bad; by her own careful account they were good, and getting better. Because showing them would mean being seen at the thing she cared about most, and being seen at the thing you care about most is, for someone with this pattern, the most exposed a person can be. The painting that means the most is the one you can least afford to have judged.

The Role Not Taken

There's a version of the held-back life that hurts in a slower way, and it shows up around leadership and responsibility.

Gabriel, whose conference invitation we met in Chapter 3, was asked twice in his career to lead a team. Both times he declined, and both times the reasons were good ones. He preferred the technical work. He didn't want the management overhead. He valued his focus. Every reason was true. None of them was the real reason. The real reason was that leading meant being visible in a way that following didn't, being the person whose decisions get scrutinized, whose judgment is on display, who can be blamed when things go wrong. The defectiveness belief, the one we named in Chapter 3, cannot abide that kind of exposure. So Gabriel stayed technical, told himself it was preference, and watched people he'd trained move into the roles he'd declined.

Years later, Gabriel admitted the cost wasn't really about status. He hadn't wanted the title for its own sake. What he grieved was that he'd never found out whether he could have done it. The pattern hadn't just cost him a role. It had cost him the chance to discover something about himself, and that discovery, once the years had passed, wasn't available to be had anymore. Some of what avoidance costs you isn't a thing. It's a piece of self-knowledge you never got to acquire.

What Avoidance Protected

Before the action, an honest accounting, because this chapter could otherwise tip into making you feel worse, and that isn't the point.

The holding back protected you. This matters. Every refusal in your history bought you something real. The job not applied for protected you from the possible rejection of not getting it. The idea not shared protected you from the possible silence after you said it. The talent kept hidden protected the thing you love from the judgment that might have tarnished it. The pattern isn't stupid. It's a careful, lifelong strategy for keeping you safe from a specific pain, and it has succeeded at that, over and over.

The accounting that matters is the one that holds both columns. What the avoidance protected, and what it cost. Most readers have only ever looked at one column, usually neither, because looking at all has felt too much. Looking at both, honestly, is the work of this chapter.

An Inventory of Both

Here is the first action.

Draw two columns. Label one *what holding back has protected me from.* Label the other *what holding back has cost me.*

In the first column, be genuinely fair to the pattern. Write what the holding back has saved you from. The rejections you didn't have to feel. The judgments you didn't have to face. The exposures you didn't have to survive. Give the pattern its due. It earned it.

In the second column, write what it cost. The roles. The friendships. The ideas. The version of your work, your ambition, your self-expression that never quite came out. Be honest, but be kind. This isn't an indictment. It's an inventory.

Then sit with both columns. The point isn't to decide the pattern was wrong. The point is to see, clearly, the trade you've been making without quite choosing it. Once you can see the trade, you can start, in small ways, to make a different one.

Name One Want

Here is the second action, smaller and more important.

Name one thing you want that you've been holding back from. Just one. Write it down in plain words. *I want to apply for that kind of role. I want to show someone my writing. I want to say the idea in the meeting. I want to ask that person to coffee.*

Naming a want is, for many readers, harder than it sounds. The pattern has spent years keeping your wants quiet, because a named want is a thing that can be disappointed. An unnamed want is safer.

So naming one, on a page, in your own words, is itself a small act against the pattern.

Then, this week, take one tiny visible action toward it. Not the whole thing. The smallest possible step. Open the application and fill in one field. Show one paragraph to one person. Say one idea in one meeting. The step should be small enough that the push can't fully block it, and visible enough that it counts as being seen, even a little.

The size of the step doesn't matter. The visibility does. You're not trying to fix the pattern this week. You're proving to yourself, in one small instance, that being seen at something you want is survivable. That's the whole assignment.

One more thing, because the pattern will try to undercut this before you've started. When you take the small visible step, the belief will be ready with a downgrade. If it goes well, it'll say the step was too small to count. If it goes badly, it'll say you should have known better than to try. Notice the downgrade when it comes, the way you've been learning to notice the critic since Chapter 5. The downgrade is not an assessment of the step. It's the pattern protecting itself, because a successful small step is a genuine threat to a belief that has organized your whole life around not taking them. Let the step count. You took it. That, this week, is enough.

In a Nutshell

The avoidant pattern doesn't only cost you closeness. It shrinks the footprint of your whole life. The job not applied for, the idea not shared, the talent kept hidden, each one small, each one explainable, together producing a life lived at half volume. The holding back protected you, genuinely, from real pain. It also cost you the fuller version of nearly everything. The work isn't to indict the pattern but to see the trade you've been making, and to start, in tiny visible steps, to make a different one. Name one want this week. Take one small visible action toward it. Being seen at something you want is survivable. The step proves it, and the proof, gathered one small step at a time, is what slowly gives you back the volume the pattern turned down.

Chapter 10 Turning Down the Critic

Marcel spent the first six months of trying to change by being harder on himself, and it made everything worse.

He had read about the pattern. He'd recognized himself in it. He'd decided, with real determination, to do something about it. And the thing he decided to do, because it was the only method he'd ever known, was to push himself. He set himself targets. Speak up in every meeting. Say yes to every invitation. Stop being so quiet. When he failed to meet the targets, which was often, he did what he'd always done. He told himself off.

The telling-off was familiar. It was, in fact, the foreman, the critic he'd named back when he started this work. Marcel had simply pointed the foreman at the new project. Where the foreman had once criticized him for being too quiet, it now also criticized him for failing to stop being too quiet. He'd given his harshest inner voice a new job, and the new job was supervising his recovery.

Six months in, Marcel was more exhausted, more ashamed, and no less avoidant than when he'd started. He'd been trying to beat the pattern out of himself, and the beating was the pattern.

When he described this to me, he asked a question that many readers eventually ask. *If pushing harder doesn't work, what does?* The answer surprised him, because it sounded soft, and Marcel did not trust soft. The answer was kindness. Not as a sentiment. As a method.

If you've spent years trying to fix yourself by being hard on yourself, and found that the hardness only dug the hole deeper, this chapter is for you.

Here is the principle. Shame doesn't loosen under pressure. It tightens. You cannot punish yourself into becoming someone who feels safe being seen, because the punishment is the same force that taught you to hide in the first place. The thing that actually loosens shame is the thing the pattern has least of, which is kindness, applied steadily, to yourself, on purpose. Kindness isn't the reward at the end of change. It's the method that makes change possible.

Why Pressure Backfires

This is worth understanding clearly, because most readers have spent their whole lives believing the opposite.

The belief goes like this. If I'm hard enough on myself, I'll improve. The harshness is what keeps my standards high. If I went easy on myself, I'd fall apart, get lazy, let myself off the hook. The critic, in this belief, is the thing holding the whole operation together.

The research on self-criticism finds close to the reverse. Compassion-focused therapy literature describes harsh self-criticism as part of a threat-based pattern that can increase shame, fear, and avoidance rather than reliably producing change (Gilbert, 2009). The harshness doesn't raise your performance. It raises your fear. And fear, for someone with this pattern, produces more hiding, not less.

Self-compassion research finds the same thing from the other direction. Neff's self-compassion framework describes self-kindness, common humanity, and mindful awareness as alternatives to harsh self-judgment, isolation, and over-identification with painful thoughts (Neff, 2003). This isn't because kindness feels nicer, though it does. It's because kindness lowers the threat level, and a lower threat level is what lets you do the frightening thing. You step toward what scares you more easily when the inner environment you're stepping from is safe.

Marcel had been trying to make himself braver by making his inner world more dangerous. It can't work. You can't frighten someone into courage.

There's a physical layer to this worth knowing, because it makes the whole thing less mysterious. In compassion-focused therapy terms, harsh self-attack can activate threat-based emotional responding. Your physiology may brace. And a braced, threatened body is built for one thing, which is defense, which for someone with this pattern means hiding. So every time you lash yourself toward courage, you trip the exact alarm that produces retreat. Compassion-focused therapy describes compassion as linked with safeness and warmth, a state that can make exploration and social risk feel more possible (Gilbert, 2009). You are not choosing between being soft and being effective. You are choosing which inner system to run, and only one of them lets you do the brave thing.

Kindness Is Not Softness

A misunderstanding I want to clear up early, because it stops a lot of readers, especially the Marcels.

Self-kindness isn't going easy on yourself. It isn't lowering your standards, making excuses, or letting yourself off the hook. That's the caricature the critic offers, because the critic wants you to believe that the only alternative to harshness is collapse.

Real self-kindness is closer to how a good coach treats an athlete they believe in. The good coach is honest about what went wrong. They don't pretend the missed shot went in. But they deliver the honesty from a position of fundamental belief in the person, with the goal of helping them do better, not with contempt. The athlete leaves the conversation wanting to try again. That's the test.

Harshness leaves you wanting to hide. Kindness leaves you wanting to try again.

So when this chapter talks about turning down the critic, it doesn't mean replacing accurate self-assessment with empty reassurance. It means changing the voice that delivers the assessment from one that wants to punish you to one that wants you to be okay.

The Three Parts of Kindness

It helps to know what self-compassion is actually made of, because the word can sound vague until you break it down. The researcher who has studied it most closely describes three parts (Neff, 2003), and all three matter for this pattern.

The first part is self-kindness, which is simply the choice to respond to your own difficulty with warmth rather than attack. It's the friend voice we'll get to in a moment. It's the opposite of the audit.

The second part is common humanity, and it's the one readers with this pattern most often miss. Common humanity is the recognition that struggling, failing, and falling short are not marks of your particular defectiveness. They're part of being a person. Everyone has them. The defectiveness belief insists your struggles are uniquely yours, proof that you specifically are not okay. Common humanity answers that the thing you're ashamed of is, in fact, one of the most universal experiences there is. You are not failing at being human. You are doing the human thing, which includes failing sometimes.

The third part is a kind of balanced attention, holding your difficulty in view without either suppressing it or drowning in it. You don't pretend the hard thing didn't happen, and you don't let it become the whole sky. You see it clearly, at its actual size.

For someone with this pattern, the common humanity piece often does the most work, because the defectiveness belief is built precisely on the conviction that you are alone in your flaw. Remembering that you're not, that the very thing you hide is shared by nearly everyone, is a quiet and powerful counter to the belief that has run the show.

Changed by Getting Kinder

Marcel's turn came slowly, and it's worth telling, because it shows what the change actually looks like, which is less dramatic than people expect.

After the exhausting six months of pushing, Marcel tried, almost reluctantly, the opposite. When he failed to speak up in a meeting, instead of the foreman's audit, he tried saying to himself what he'd say to a colleague. *That was a hard room. You'll get the next one.* It felt false at first. He didn't believe it. He said it anyway, because the alternative had already failed.

What he noticed, over a couple of months, was not a surge of confidence. It was something smaller. He started dreading meetings slightly less. The dread had been fed, he realized, not by the meetings themselves but by the audit that always followed them. When the audit softened, the dread had less fuel. And when the dread had less fuel, he found himself, occasionally, speaking up, not because he'd forced himself, but because the cost of speaking had quietly dropped. The kindness hadn't motivated him. It had lowered the threat, and the lowered threat had freed him. He'd spent his whole life believing the foreman was what kept his standards up. It turned out the foreman had mostly just been keeping him quiet.

The Friend Standard

The simplest tool for this is one you already own. You use it on other people constantly. You just don't point it at yourself.

When a friend you love fails at something, or embarrasses themselves, or doesn't get the thing they wanted, you don't pile on. You don't list their flaws. You don't tell them it confirms what you always suspected about them. You're warm. You're accurate but gentle. You remind them, in some form, that they're okay, that the failure isn't the whole story, that you still think well of them.

You have, in other words, a kind voice. It's fully developed. It's wise and warm and good at this. You just reserve it for other people.

The reframe is to borrow that voice for yourself. The next time the critic delivers its verdict on something you did, ask one question. *What would I say to a friend who told me they'd done this exact thing?* Then say that to yourself. Not as a trick. As a genuine redirection of a capacity you already have toward a target you've always excluded.

Valeria, whose friendships we touched on in Chapter 3, tried this for the first time after a work presentation she felt had gone badly. Her critic was running its usual audit. She stopped and asked what she'd say to a colleague who'd given the same presentation and felt the same way. The answer arrived instantly, because the kind voice was already there. *You were nervous and you still got through it, the content was solid, one awkward moment isn't what people remember.* She was startled by how different it felt to receive that, in her own head, than to receive the audit. It didn't erase the audit. It just sat beside it, truer.

A Small Kindness Practice

Here is the first action of this chapter.

This week, when you catch yourself in a moment of self-criticism, do three small things, in order.

First, notice the criticism, the way we practiced in Chapter 5. *That's the critic.* You already know how to do this part.

Second, put a hand somewhere on yourself, if you're somewhere you can. The chest, the arm, wherever. This sounds strange and it works. Physical warmth, even your own, signals safety to the part of you that's braced. You don't have to believe in it for it to do something.

Third, ask the friend question. *What would I say to someone I cared about who was in this exact spot?* And say that, inwardly, to yourself.

That's the whole practice. Notice, warmth, friend question. It takes thirty seconds. Do it once a day this week, whenever the critic shows up. You're not trying to silence the critic. You're building a different response to it, one repetition at a time.

The Critic Will Protest

You should know what happens when you first try this, so it doesn't throw you.

The critic does not welcome the kinder voice. The first few times you offer yourself the friend question, the critic will often get louder, not quieter. It will tell you the kindness is self-indulgent. It will tell you you're making excuses, going soft, lowering the bar that has kept you from becoming truly worthless. It may get briefly nastier than usual, the way any old authority does when its power is questioned for the first time.

This protest is not a sign that the kindness is wrong. It's a sign that the kindness is working, that it has been registered as a genuine challenge to the established order. The critic has run your inner world for a long time. It is not going to cede ground quietly. Expect the protest. When it comes, you can even name it. *The critic doesn't like that I'm trying this. Of course it doesn't.* That sentence alone puts you outside the critic, watching it object, rather than inside it, obeying.

Over weeks, the protest fades. Not because you defeated the critic in argument, which we established in Chapter 5 doesn't work, but because the kinder voice kept showing up anyway, and the part of you that was braced began, slowly, to believe it was allowed. The critic gets quieter not when it loses the argument but when it stops being the only voice in the room.

One Kind Thing on Purpose

Here is the second action, and the simplest in the book.

This week, do one small kind thing for yourself, on purpose, and let yourself notice you're doing it.

Not a grand gesture. Not a reward you have to earn. A small thing, done deliberately, as an act of treating yourself as someone worth treating well. Make the good coffee instead of the quick coffee. Take the walk you'd normally skip. Go to bed early without calling it lazy. Cancel the thing you dread and don't make yourself pay for the cancellation with guilt.

The point isn't the thing. The point is the on-purpose. You're practicing, in one small instance, treating yourself the way the kind voice would treat you. The pattern has spent years treating you as someone who has to earn good treatment. This week, once, give it without the earning.

This is the foundation the rest of the book is built on. The chapters ahead ask you to do frightening things, to be seen, to stay close, to step toward what you want. You can only do frightening things from a safe base. The kindness is the base. Build it first, and build it before you think you've earned it, because the whole trap of this pattern is the belief that kindness is something you have to earn. You don't. You get to start being on your own side today, exactly as you are, unfinished and afraid and trying. That is not the reward for finishing the work. It is the condition that lets the work begin.

In a Nutshell

You cannot punish yourself into change. Shame tightens under pressure and loosens under kindness. The harshness you've aimed at yourself for years hasn't raised your performance; it's raised your fear, and fear produces more hiding, not less. Self-kindness isn't softness or lowered standards. It's the honest, warm voice you already use on people you love, finally pointed at yourself. Borrow that voice. Ask what you'd say to a friend, and say it to yourself. Do one kind thing on purpose this week. Kindness isn't the reward at the end of change. It's the base that makes change possible.

Chapter 11 Letting Yourself Be Seen

Hugo decided, one ordinary Tuesday, to answer a question honestly, and it changed less than he feared and more than he expected.

The question was *how was your weekend.* A colleague asked it in the office kitchen, the way people do, not expecting much. Hugo's standard answer to this question, refined over decades, was *good thanks, you?* The answer was designed to be frictionless. It gave nothing away. It returned the question so the other person could talk instead. It got Hugo out of the kitchen.

This Tuesday, for reasons he couldn't fully explain, Hugo answered differently. He said his weekend had actually been a bit lonely, that he'd meant to see people and hadn't, and that he was trying to be better about that. He said it lightly. It took about eight seconds.

He braced for the cost. The cost, in his imagination, was that the colleague would find the honesty strange, would not know what to do with it, would file Hugo under *overshares in the kitchen.*

What actually happened was that the colleague paused, said *honestly, same, weekends are hard when you live alone,* and the two of them had a real two-minute conversation that neither had expected. Hugo walked back to his desk having been, for eight seconds, slightly more visible than usual, and having survived it. More than survived it. The small visibility had bought him a small connection. The thing he'd spent decades avoiding had, this once, given him exactly what he wanted.

If you've ever given the frictionless answer when a truer one was right there, and felt the small flatness of having stayed hidden again, this chapter is for you.

Here is the principle. Being seen isn't an ordeal to endure. It's an experiment to run. You don't have to force yourself into big, frightening exposures and white-knuckle through them. You take one small, chosen step toward being visible, and you treat what happens next as information, not as a verdict on your worth. The fear says visibility is a test you'll fail. The experiment treats visibility as a question you're genuinely curious about. That shift, from test to experiment, is the whole chapter.

Experiments, Not Ordeals

I want to be careful about a word, because the wrong version of this chapter has hurt people.

There's an approach to fear that says the way through is exposure. Force yourself into the frightening situation, stay until the fear comes down, repeat. For some fears, in the right hands, that approach has solid evidence behind it. But for many readers with this pattern, exposure framed as an ordeal backfires. You grit your teeth, push yourself into something exposing, and the part of you that's been protecting you experiences the whole thing as a confirmation that the world is dangerous and you had to brace to survive it. You did the brave thing and came out more convinced you needed the wall.

So this chapter doesn't ask for ordeals. It asks for experiments. The difference is not the size of the step. It's the stance.

An ordeal is something you endure to prove you can. The goal is survival. You white-knuckle through and feel relieved when it's over.

An experiment is something you try to find out what happens. The goal is information. You're genuinely curious about the result, and any result teaches you something.

When Hugo answered the kitchen question honestly, he wasn't enduring an ordeal. He was, almost by accident, running an experiment. The hypothesis his fear had always offered was *if I'm honest, it'll go badly.* He tested it, once, in a low-stakes setting. The result was data. The data didn't match the fear. One piece of data doesn't overturn a lifelong belief, but it's a start, and it was gathered through curiosity rather than endurance, which is why it stuck.

Being Seen Is Also Wanted

There's a piece of this that the language of fear can hide, and it matters, so let me say it plainly. You don't only fear being seen. You also want it.

The whole pattern, the quiet distance we've been tracing since the first chapter, is built on a longing as much as a fear. The longing to be known. To have someone see the real version and stay. To stop performing the frictionless answer and offer the true one and have it be received. That longing is not weakness, and it isn't going away. It's the thing the experiments are in service of. You're not running visibility experiments to toughen yourself up. You're running them to get, in small survivable doses, the thing you've wanted all along and been too frightened to reach for.

This is why the experiments feel different from exposure. Exposure is about reducing fear. Experiments, in the way this chapter means them, are about reaching toward something you actually want. Hugo didn't answer the kitchen question honestly to practice tolerating discomfort. He did it, in some part of himself, because he was tired of the frictionless answer and wanted, just once, for someone to know how his weekend had actually been. The wanting was the engine. Let your wanting be the engine too. It will take you further than discipline ever could.

Results Are Information, Not Verdicts

Here is the part that makes the experiment stance work, and it's worth slowing down for.

When you run a visibility experiment, the result is information about that situation. It is not a verdict on you.

This matters because the defectiveness belief will try to convert every result into a verdict. If the experiment goes well, the belief says it was luck or politeness. If it goes badly, the belief says it confirms what you always knew. Either way, the belief tries to make the result about your fundamental worth.

The experiment stance refuses the conversion. A visibility experiment that goes well tells you that, in that situation, being seen went well. A visibility experiment that goes badly tells you that, in that situation, being seen didn't land, for reasons that might have nothing to do with you, the other person's bad day, the wrong moment, a genuine mismatch. Neither result is a verdict. Both are information. You're a scientist gathering data about a question, not a defendant awaiting a sentence.

Clara, whose unsent job application we met in Chapter 9, eventually applied for a role like the one in her tab. She didn't get it. The old pattern would have read the rejection as proof. *See. I was right not to try. I'm not good enough.* The experiment stance let her read it differently. She'd run an experiment, and the data was that this particular role, with this particular pool of candidates, didn't break her way. She applied for two more. She got the second. The rejection had been information, not a verdict, and treating it that way was what let her keep going.

How to Design Your Own

A good visibility experiment has four features. It's small. It's chosen by you, not imposed. It's specific. And it has a result you can actually observe.

Small means small enough that you can imagine actually doing it. Not the biggest exposure you can think of. The smallest one that still counts as being seen. If a public talk is a ten, you're not looking for a nine. You're looking for a two.

Chosen means you pick it. This isn't a list of assignments. The experiments that work are the ones you design for your own life, in an area you actually care about. Nobody is grading you. There's no curriculum.

Specific means you know exactly what the action is. Not *be more open.* That's not an experiment; it's a wish. *Tell one colleague one true thing about my weekend* is an experiment. You know if you did it.

Observable means you can see what happens. The point is to gather data, so the experiment should produce some. Did you say the thing? What happened when you did? How did it actually feel afterward, not how you predicted it would feel?

Some examples readers have used, all small, all chosen, all specific. Saying a real opinion in a conversation where you'd normally stay neutral. Posting one thing you made. Wearing something you like but usually consider too noticeable. Answering *how are you* with one true sentence. Asking one person one question you'd normally swallow. Sitting with the group at lunch instead of at your desk, once.

None of these is brave in any visible way. Each is, for someone with this pattern, a small act of letting yourself be seen. That's exactly the size we want.

Build Your Own Ladder

One experiment is a start. What changes a life is a sequence of them, arranged so each one makes the next slightly possible.

Think of it as a ladder you build yourself. At the bottom are the experiments so small they barely register as risks. Saying a real opinion to one safe person. Higher up are ones that cost a little more. Sharing something you made with one person whose response matters to you. Higher still are the ones that would frighten you today and won't frighten you nearly as much after you've climbed the lower rungs. You don't start at the top. You start at the bottom, on a rung you can actually reach, and you climb only as fast as the climbing stays survivable.

The mistake the ordeal approach makes is sending people to the top of the ladder first, on the theory that the biggest fear is the one to attack. For this pattern, that usually produces a fall, and a fall confirms the belief. The ladder approach lets each rung build the footing for the next. By the time you reach a rung that would have terrified you at the start, you're a different climber, because the lower rungs taught your body that being seen can go fine.

You build the ladder for your own life. Nobody else can rank your rungs, because nobody else knows which acts of visibility cost you what. The painting is a low rung for one person and the highest rung in the world for another. Rank your own.

A Painting Shown

Noemi, whose hidden paintings we met in Chapter 9, built a ladder without quite calling it that.

Her bottom rung was almost absurdly small. She left one painting visible in her flat when a friend came over, instead of putting it away as she always had. She said nothing about it. The friend noticed it, said it was beautiful, asked if Noemi knew the artist. Noemi said, barely, that she'd made it. The friend was delighted. That was the whole experiment. It took ten seconds of not hiding, and the result was one piece of data that contradicted a decade of the belief's predictions.

The next rung, weeks later, was showing a friend a painting on purpose. The rung after that, months later, was letting two paintings hang in a friend's cafe for a month. She did not, in the time I knew of her work, have a gallery show or sell anything or become a public artist. That was never the point. The point was that the thing she loved most had come out of hiding, one survivable rung at a time, and that she was no longer carrying it alone in a spare room. The ladder she built was short and entirely hers, and it changed her relationship to the thing she cared about most.

The Kind Debrief

Here is a step most people skip, and it's the one that makes the experiments compound.

After you run an experiment, debrief it. Kindly. The way a good scientist reviews a result, or a good coach reviews a game. Not the way the critic would.

Ask three questions. What did I actually do? What actually happened, as opposed to what I feared would happen? What did I learn?

Keep the debrief honest and warm. If the experiment went well, let it count. Don't let the belief downgrade it to luck. If it went badly, don't let the belief inflate it to a verdict. Either way, you ran the experiment, which is the part that matters, because the running is the thing that's new.

Write the debrief down if you can. Over weeks, a record of small experiments and their actual results becomes the most powerful counter-evidence you have against the defectiveness belief. The belief has been making claims about what happens when you're seen. The record shows what actually happens. The record usually disagrees with the belief. That disagreement, accumulated, is how the belief begins to lose its grip. Avoidance keeps the belief alive by making sure it's never tested (Clark & Wells, 1995). The experiment tests it. The testing, gently and repeatedly, is the work.

One more thing about the debrief, because it's where the pattern tries to sneak back in. Pay particular attention to the gap between what you predicted and what happened. Before the experiment, your fear made a prediction. *They'll think it's strange. It'll be awkward. They'll judge me.* After the experiment, you have the actual result. Almost always, the gap is large, and the actual result is gentler than the prediction. That gap is the single most useful thing the debrief produces. It's direct evidence that your fear is a poor forecaster, that it systematically predicts worse than what occurs. Once you've seen that gap a dozen times, you start to trust the forecaster a little less, which means the next experiment costs a little less to run.

Run One This Week

Your action this week is one experiment. One.

Design it yourself, using the four features. Small, chosen, specific, observable. Pick an area you actually care about. Pick a step small enough that you can imagine doing it, and visible enough that it counts as being seen.

Run it once. Then do the kind debrief. What did you do, what actually happened, what did you learn.

That's all. Not a program. Not a campaign. One small chosen experiment, run with curiosity, debriefed with kindness. Schema therapy includes behavioral pattern-breaking, and trial evidence supports schema therapy as an effective treatment for several personality-disorder presentations; the small experiment here is a self-help adaptation of that broader principle (Bamelis et al., 2014). You're not enduring anything. You're finding something out. Let yourself be a little curious about what you find.

In a Nutshell

Being seen isn't an ordeal to endure. It's an experiment to run. The difference isn't the size of the step; it's the stance. An ordeal is survived. An experiment is run, with curiosity, to find something out. Design your own, small and chosen and specific. Treat the result as information, never as a verdict on your worth, because the belief will try to convert it and the experiment refuses. Then debrief kindly. A record of small experiments and their actual results is the strongest counter-evidence you have, because avoidance keeps the fear alive by making sure it's never tested. Run one experiment this week. Be curious about what you find.

Chapter 12 Staying When You Want to Run

Six months after the Sunday lunch where his wall went up, Mateo did something he had never done before. He went back.

You'll remember Mateo from earlier chapters. The friend who texts Felix twice a year. The man whose wall rose in conflict, who answered his partner's first hard question with flat, short, technically-responsive words that were in no way truthful, and who didn't tell his partner this for six months.

What changed at six months was small. His partner asked another hard question, a different one, and Mateo felt the familiar thing happen. The signal to flee. The wall starting up. The lively part of him preparing to leave the room while his body stayed in the chair. He'd felt it a hundred times. This time, he'd been doing the work in this book for a few months, and he noticed it as it happened. *The wall is going up.* He named it, the way Chapter 6 had taught him.

Naming it didn't stop it. He still went quiet. He still gave a short answer. He still felt himself pull back behind the glass. The wall did what the wall does.

But an hour later, instead of letting the moment pass into the six-month silence the way he always had, Mateo went back. He found his partner in the kitchen and said something he'd never said. *I'm sorry, I went somewhere just now. I do that when things get hard. It's not about you. I'm trying to learn how to stay.* It took ten seconds and cost him more than the whole rest of the day. His partner, who had spent years quietly wondering what they'd done wrong every time Mateo went flat, started to cry, and then they had the realest conversation of their relationship.

If you've felt the reflex to vanish when things get close, and watched yourself act on it again and again, this chapter is for you.

Here is the principle. You don't have to stop wanting to run. The urge to flee is wired deep, built early, and it isn't going to disappear because you read a book. What you can learn is to come back. The wall will go up. You'll still go quiet sometimes, still pull behind the glass. The work isn't to never rupture. It's to repair. And the repair, it turns out, matters far more than the rupture ever did.

The Urge to Flee Is Not the Problem

Most readers, by this point in the book, are hoping for the chapter that finally makes the urge to run go away. This isn't that chapter, and I want to be honest about why.

The urge to flee when things get close is the wall, which we met in Chapter 6, doing exactly what it was built to do. It was built early, in conditions that made it necessary, and it's been on duty for decades. It will not be retired by an act of will. For a long time, possibly always, you'll feel the pull to vanish when closeness rises past a certain threshold. Expecting yourself to never feel it is setting yourself up to fail, and then to use the failure as more evidence against yourself. We're not doing that.

So we change the target. The target isn't *never feel the urge.* The target is *come back after you act on it.* This is a much kinder goal, and a much more achievable one, and it happens to be the one that actually changes relationships.

Here's the reason it works. The thing that damages closeness isn't the moment you pull away. People can handle a partner or friend who goes quiet sometimes. What damages closeness is the pulling away that's never named, never returned from, never repaired, so that the other person is left to invent a story about what they did wrong. Mateo's partner didn't suffer most from the flat answers.

They suffered from the six months of silence after them, in which they had to guess.

Repair Is the Skill

Rupture and repair is a pattern that runs through every close relationship, healthy ones included. The healthiest relationships aren't the ones without rupture. They're the ones that repair well.

The therapy literature gives one useful analogy here. Work on the therapeutic alliance defines ruptures as strains in the bond or collaboration between therapist and client, and repair of those ruptures is associated with better treatment outcomes (Eubanks et al., 2018). The repair does something the unbroken connection can't. It teaches both people that the relationship can survive a rupture, which is exactly the thing someone with this pattern has never been sure of.

For you, this is freeing. It means you don't have to become someone who never withdraws. You couldn't, anyway. It means you have to become someone who repairs. And repair is a skill, which means it can be learned, practiced, and done badly at first and better later.

Why Repair Feels Impossible at First

If repair is so simple, you might wonder why people with this pattern find it so hard. The answer is worth understanding, because it explains why the first repair costs so much and the tenth costs almost nothing.

Repair requires going back toward the exact thing you withdrew from. The whole point of the wall was to get away from a moment that felt unsafe. Repair means turning around and walking back into it, on purpose, after you've already escaped. Every instinct the pattern has built says this is madness. You got out. Why would you go back in?

There's also the belief, doing its work. The defectiveness belief predicts that if you go back and name your withdrawal, the other person will use it against you. They'll confirm that you're difficult, too much, not worth the trouble. Repair, to the belief, is handing the other person a loaded weapon. So the pattern keeps you away from repair with the same force it uses to keep you away from everything else that risks being seen.

This is why the first repair feels enormous and looks tiny. Inside, you're overriding a lifetime of training and ignoring a belief that's screaming. Outside, you're saying one honest sentence in a kitchen. The gap between the internal cost and the external size is the whole difficulty. Knowing the gap is there helps. When the repair feels impossibly large, remind yourself that the largeness is internal, that what you're actually about to do is small and ordinary, and that the size you're feeling is the pattern's estimate, not the real one.

What Repair Actually Sounds Like

Repair is simpler than most readers fear. It isn't a grand emotional performance. It's usually a few honest sentences, delivered after the fact.

A repair has roughly three parts, though you don't have to hit them mechanically. You name what happened. You take your part without excessive apology. You say something true about wanting to stay connected.

Mateo's repair had all three in ten seconds. *I went somewhere just now* names it. *I do that when things get hard, it's not about you* takes his part without collapsing into self-attack. *I'm trying to learn how to stay* says the true thing about wanting the connection. He didn't plan it as three parts. He just said the honest thing. The structure was underneath.

Notice what the repair is not. It's not a lengthy self-criticism. It's not *I'm so sorry, I'm terrible at this, I always ruin everything, you deserve better.* That version, which the critic would write for you, isn't repair. It's the pattern in a new costume, pulling the focus onto your unworthiness and asking the other person to reassure you. Real repair stays simple and faces outward, toward the connection, not inward, toward the verdict.

Staying a Little Longer

Before the repair, there's an earlier skill worth building, which is staying in the room a little longer than the urge wants you to.

You won't always manage this, and that's fine; that's what repair is for. But sometimes, when you catch the wall rising early, the way Chapter 6 taught you, you have a small window. In that window, instead of leaving, you can try staying for one more beat. Not for the whole hard conversation. For one more sentence. One more minute. A little longer than the urge wanted.

Eloise, whose ideas die in meetings, used this in a different arena. When the urge to go quiet rose, she'd try to stay present for just one more contribution before she let herself retreat. One sentence past where she'd normally have gone silent. It was small. Over months, the one-more-sentence habit meaningfully changed how present she was at work, because the staying compounded the way the leaving used to.

The plan is simple. When you feel the wall rising, see if you can stay for one more beat than the urge wants. If you can't, that's fine. The repair is still available. But sometimes you can, and the staying, a little at a time, stretches what you're able to be present for. Think of it as widening the window by a second at a time.

You're not trying to throw the window open. You're easing it up, a fraction, more often than you used to, until one day you notice the room has more air in it than it used to have.

Repair Works in Friendship Too

Repair isn't only for partners. It's often most needed in the friendships that quietly faded.

Mateo, after the repair with his partner went better than he'd feared, did something he'd been not-doing for eight years. He texted Felix. Not a casual twice-a-year text. A real one. He wrote that he was sorry they'd drifted, that he'd always valued the friendship and had been bad at showing it, and that he'd like to catch up properly if Felix was open to it. He almost didn't send it. The push, which we met in Chapter 8, built its case in the usual way. Felix is probably busy. It's been too long. He'll find it strange.

Felix replied within the hour. He'd been wondering, for years, whether he'd done something to cause the distance. Mateo's message was, for Felix, a small repair of a rupture Felix hadn't even known the cause of. They met the following week. The friendship didn't snap instantly back to what it had been at eight years old, because friendships don't, but it reopened, which is all a repair is for. The drift had been held in place by one man's push and the other man's reasonable decision to give him space. One honest message undid years of it.

If the Repair Isn't Met Well

An honest caution, because the belief will want to know about this.

Sometimes a repair isn't met warmly. You go back, you say the honest thing, and the other person is cool, or hurt, or not ready to receive it. This is the outcome the pattern is most afraid of, and it does happen.

Here's what to hold on to if it does. A repair that isn't met well is still worth having made. You did your part. You named what happened and reached back toward connection. The other person's response is theirs, shaped by their own history, their own day, their own capacity in that moment. It is information about where the relationship is, not a verdict on you, the same distinction we drew in the last chapter. Some relationships won't have room for your repair, and a few of those will be relationships it's worth grieving and letting go. But the skill you practiced by making the repair is yours to keep, and you'll carry it into the relationships that do have room. Don't let one cool response teach the pattern that repair is dangerous. The repair was right. The reception was just one more piece of data.

When You Withdraw, Come Back

Here is the action for this chapter, and it's the one I most want you to try.

This week, you will, at some point, withdraw. You'll go quiet, go flat, pull behind the glass, give the short answer when a real one was needed. It's going to happen, because it always happens, and this week we're going to use it.

When it happens, come back. Not in the moment, necessarily; in the moment the wall is up and you may not be able to. Later. An hour later, a day later. Go back to the person and say one honest thing about it.

It can be small. *Sorry, I went a bit quiet earlier, I do that sometimes when things matter.* That's a complete repair. You don't have to explain the whole pattern. You don't have to have the big conversation. One honest sentence, delivered after a withdrawal, to the person you withdrew from. That's the entire assignment.

The first time will cost you more than it should. Repair, for someone who has spent a life vanishing, feels enormous. It looks, from the outside, like almost nothing. That gap, between how big it feels and how small it looks, is the gap you're learning to cross. Cross it once this week. One return. One honest sentence. See what happens.

There's one more reason repair matters, and it reaches back to Chapter 7. When you withdraw and then return, you're not only repairing with the other person. You're showing the younger you something they never got to learn. That a rupture doesn't have to mean abandonment. That someone can go away and come back. That connection can survive a break. The younger you, who learned that distance was permanent and that the safest move was to leave first, gets to watch the adult you demonstrate, in real time, that the old rule isn't the only rule. Every repair you make is also a quiet message to the part of you that learned to hide. *It's safe to come back now. I'll show you how.*

In a Nutshell

You don't have to stop wanting to run. The urge to flee was built early and won't disappear because you decided it should. What you can learn is to come back. The rupture, the going quiet, the pulling away, isn't what damages closeness. What damages closeness is the withdrawal that's never named or repaired, leaving the other person to invent a story about what they did wrong. Repair is a skill: name what happened, take your part without excessive apology, say the true thing about wanting to stay connected. The healthiest relationships aren't the ones without rupture. They're the ones that repair. This week, when you withdraw, come back, and say one honest thing. And remember, as you do it, that the return is also a message to the younger you, who needs to learn that going away and coming back is something a person is allowed to do.

Chapter 13 Living by What Matters and Holding Steady

Clara went to her daughter's school play, and she sat in the front row, and that was the whole victory.

To anyone else in the auditorium, a mother sitting near the front at a school play was not an event. It was the most ordinary thing in the world. For Clara, who had spent most of her daughter's childhood choosing seats near the back, near the exit, where she could watch without being watched, the front row was a small act of a different kind of life.

She hadn't stopped being afraid. That's the part worth noticing. Sitting near the front, she felt the old discomfort fully. The sense of being visible. The quiet certainty that other parents were noticing her, assessing her, finding her somehow not quite right. The fear hadn't gone anywhere. What had changed was that Clara had decided, in advance, that being a mother who showed up fully for her daughter mattered more to her than being comfortable. So she sat near the front, afraid, and she stayed there, and her daughter found her face from the stage in the first thirty seconds and beamed, and that was the whole thing.

Clara told me afterward that the fear during the play had been almost exactly as strong as it would have been ten years earlier. The work she'd done hadn't made the front row comfortable. What it had done was make the front row possible while uncomfortable. She'd stopped waiting to feel ready. She'd acted from what mattered, and let the fear come along for the ride.

If you've spent your life waiting to feel ready before you do the things that matter, and noticed that ready never quite arrives, this chapter is for you.

Here is the principle. For most of this book, the work has been about reducing fear, softening the critic, lowering the wall. This chapter changes the question. The question is no longer only what you want to stop. It's who you want to be. And the truth that holds this final stretch together is that you don't have to wait for the fear to go before you start living by what matters. You act from your values with the fear still present. The fear stops being the thing that decides.

The Question Changes

Up to now, this book has mostly been about subtraction. Less critic. Less wall. Less of the belief's grip. That work matters, and you should keep doing it. But a life built only on subtraction is a strange, thin thing. You can spend years successfully reducing your fear and still have no idea what you're reducing it for.

So the question changes here, from what you want less of to what you want more of. Not what you're moving away from. What you're moving toward.

This is the shift from managing a problem to building a life. People who only ever work on reducing their symptoms often find that even when the symptoms ease, they're left facing a kind of emptiness, because they organized everything around the problem and never decided what they actually wanted the freed-up space to hold. The reduction was supposed to be in service of something. This chapter is about naming the something.

The approach that has studied this most carefully treats values not as lofty ideals but as directions you choose to move in, regardless of how you feel on a given day (Hayes et al., 2012). A value isn't a goal you complete. It's a direction you keep heading. Being a present parent isn't a box you tick; it's a direction Clara can keep choosing, play after play, year after year. Naming your directions is what lets you act even when the fear is loud, because you're no longer asking whether you feel ready. You're asking which way you want to be heading.

You Don't Wait for the Fear to Go

This is the part that changes lives, so I want to be plain about it.

Most people with this pattern operate on an unspoken assumption. The assumption is that one day, after enough work, the fear will lift, and then they'll do the things they've been holding back from. They'll apply for the role once they feel confident. They'll reach out once they feel ready. They'll let themselves be seen once being seen stops being frightening.

That day doesn't come. Not because the work fails, but because that's not how it works. The fear softens, over time, in response to action, not before it. If you wait for the fear to go before you act, you wait forever, because the acting is part of what loosens the fear. You have the order backward, and the backward order is itself a feature of the pattern, one more way of staying safe by staying still.

So you flip it. You act first, with the fear present, in the direction of what matters. Clara didn't sit in the front row because she'd stopped being afraid. She sat there because her daughter mattered more than her fear, and she let both things be true at once. The fear was real. The value was realer. She moved in the direction of the value and carried the fear along.

This is not the same as forcing yourself, white-knuckled, through an ordeal, which we warned against in Chapter 11. The difference is the engine. Forcing is driven by *I should be able to do this.* Value-led action is driven by *this matters to me.* The first runs on shame and burns out. The second runs on meaning and sustains. When you find yourself stuck at the edge of a frightening action, the question to ask isn't *am I ready*. It's *does this matter to me*. If it does, you can move, ready or not.

What Do You Actually Value

Here is the first reflection of this chapter, and it's worth doing slowly.

Most people have never actually been asked what they value, only what they want to achieve or avoid. So this can feel unfamiliar. Take it gently.

Ask yourself, in a few different areas of life, what kind of person you'd want to be, if the fear weren't casting a vote. In relationships, what would you move toward? Closeness, honesty, being known, being a good friend? In work, what would you want to stand for? Doing work that matters, being seen for it, leading, creating? In the ordinary texture of your days, what would you want more of? Warmth, presence, courage, play?

Don't answer with goals. Answer with directions. Not *get promoted* but *let myself be seen at work*. Not *get married* but *let someone close*. Not *have more friends* but *be the kind of friend who reaches out*. The goals can come later. Right now you're naming the directions you'd choose if you were choosing freely.

Write down two or three. Just two or three. These are the directions this final stretch of work is in service of. When the fear asks why you'd do something so uncomfortable, these are your answer.

Margot, whose reachable-but-not-always mother we met in Chapter 4, did this reflection and found that the direction she most wanted, underneath everything, was simply to stop performing and let a few people know the real her. She'd never named it before. Naming it gave her something to aim the rest of the work at. Every frightening small step after that had a reason attached. She wasn't being brave for its own sake. She was heading somewhere she'd chosen.

The Setback Is Coming

Now for the part most self-help books skip, and the part that determines whether change lasts.

You will have setbacks. I want to say this plainly, in advance, because the setback itself is far less dangerous than what you tend to make of it.

After a stretch of progress, you'll have a bad week. The wall will go up hard. The critic will get loud again. You'll withdraw from someone you'd been getting closer to, decline an opportunity you'd have reached for last month, fall back into the old pattern as though none of the work had happened. This is not a sign that the work failed. This is what change actually looks like. Progress is never a straight line up. It's a jagged line that trends, over time, in a direction. The jagged part is not the exception. It's the shape.

Research on schema therapy for personality disorders supports durable improvement for many patients, but it should not be read as a promise of a tidy, linear process for every person (Bamelis et al., 2014). It shows people getting better in fits and starts, sliding back, recovering, sliding back less far the next time. The slides are part of the process. They are built in.

The danger isn't the setback. The danger is the meaning the pattern assigns to it. The defectiveness belief, which we named back in Chapter 3, is always waiting for evidence, and a setback looks, to the belief, like a confirmation. *See. You haven't changed at all. It was always going to come to this. The progress was fake.* If you believe that voice, a single bad week can undo months of work, not because the bad week was powerful but because the belief used it to seize back control.

A Bad Week Is Weather, Not a Verdict

Here is the line I most want you to carry out of this chapter. A bad week is weather, not a verdict.

Weather passes. It tells you about the conditions today, not about the climate of your whole life, and certainly not about your worth. A storm doesn't mean the season has reversed. It means it's storming, today, and that it will, in time, stop. The person who treats a bad week as weather waits it out, stays kind to themselves through it, and is back on the path within days. The person who treats it as a verdict collapses, concludes the whole project was a delusion, and abandons the path entirely. Same bad week. Two completely different outcomes, decided entirely by the meaning assigned.

Marcel, whose self-compassion turn we followed in Chapter 10, had a setback about four months into real progress. A hard period at work, and suddenly the foreman was back at full volume and he was avoiding everything again. The old Marcel would have taken this as proof. The Marcel who'd done the work took it, with some effort, as weather. He said to himself, more or less, *this is a hard week, the old pattern is loud because I'm under strain, this is not a referendum on everything.* He was kind to himself through it, the way Chapter 10 had taught him. Within ten days he was back. The setback that would once have ended everything cost him a week and a half, because he refused to let it mean more than it meant.

That refusal is a skill. It's the skill of meeting a setback with kindness rather than collapse, and it's possibly the single most important thing in this chapter, because it's the thing that turns a temporary slip into a recoverable event instead of a final verdict.

Your Early Warning Signs

Here is the second reflection, and it's a practical one.

Setbacks usually announce themselves. Before you fully slide back, there are early signs, and if you know your own, you can catch the slide while it's small.

Think back over your previous slides into the old pattern, the times the wall went up hard and stayed up, the periods you withdrew. What came first? For many readers, the earliest signs are small and physical or behavioral. Sleeping a little worse. Cancelling one thing, then another. Letting messages sit unanswered. A particular tightness returning. The screen coming out more. A quiet retreat from the people you'd been getting closer to.

Name your three earliest warning signs. The earliest ones, not the late ones. By the time you're fully withdrawn, the slide is well underway. You want the signs that show up at the very start, when the slide is still small enough to interrupt.

Then, for each sign, write one kind response. Not a punishment. Not a *you're slipping again, sort yourself out.* A kind response. *I notice I'm cancelling things. That usually means I'm under strain. Let me be gentle with myself this week and reach out to one person instead of going fully quiet.* The kind response is what turns a warning sign from the start of a collapse into the start of a recovery.

A Maintenance Plan

Here is the third reflection, which pulls the others together.

A maintenance plan isn't elaborate. It's a short, personal document you write for the version of you who's having a bad week and can't think clearly. That version of you won't be able to generate wisdom from scratch. So you generate it now, while you can, and leave it where they'll find it.

Your plan can be a few lines. What your values are, the directions you've chosen, so the bad-week version remembers what this is all for. Your three earliest warning signs, so they can catch the slide early. Your kind responses to each. And one or two things that reliably help you, the grounding pause from Chapter 6, reaching out to a specific person, a particular walk, whatever you've learned works for you.

Write it on one page. Keep it somewhere you'll actually find it. You're writing a letter to your future self for the day they'll need it, and they will need it, and they'll be grateful you wrote it while the weather was clear.

One Step Toward a Value

Your action this week is one value-led step.

Look at the two or three directions you named. Pick one. Take one small step in that direction this week, with the fear fully present. Don't wait to feel ready. Apply the principle of this chapter directly. The step matters because it's in the direction you chose, not because you've stopped being afraid of it.

Make it small enough to actually do and meaningful enough to count. If your direction is letting people close, the step might be telling one person one true thing. If it's being seen at work, it might be one visible contribution. The size isn't the point. The direction is. You're proving to yourself that you can move toward what matters while afraid, which is the only way anyone ever has.

In a Nutshell

The question changes here, from what you want to stop to who you want to be. You don't wait for the fear to go before you live by what matters; you act from your values with the fear present, because the fear softens in response to action, not before it. Name two or three directions you'd choose if fear weren't voting, and let them be your answer when the fear asks why. Setbacks are coming, and they're built into how change works. A bad week is weather, not a verdict. Know your three earliest warning signs and meet each with kindness. Write a one-page plan for the version of you who'll be having a hard week. Then take one step toward a value this week, fear and all.

Chapter 14 Getting Support That Helps

Felix sat in his car outside the therapist's office for eleven minutes before he went in, and very nearly drove away twice.

He had found the therapist weeks earlier, after months of telling himself he didn't need one. He'd done the reading. He'd done the work in books like this one. He was managing. The story he told himself was that therapy was for people who couldn't manage, and he could, mostly, so it would be self-indulgent, an admission of a weakness he didn't quite have.

What had finally changed his mind was a quiet, honest recognition that the managing had a ceiling. He'd come a real distance on his own. He'd also reached a layer that the books kept gesturing at and that he couldn't seem to reach by himself, the younger part of him we talked about in Chapter 7, the original feelings underneath the belief. Every time he got close to that layer alone, he'd back away. He needed, he finally admitted, someone in the room.

So he made the appointment, and then he sat in his car for eleven minutes, because making the appointment and walking through the door turned out to be two different acts of courage. The voice in his car was loud. *This is unnecessary. You'll waste her time. She'll think there's nothing really wrong with you. She'll think there's something seriously wrong with you. You don't even know what you'd say.* He went in anyway. Forty-five minutes later he came out having felt, for the first time he could remember, that he'd been seen by someone whose job was to see him, and that it had been a relief rather than a danger.

If the idea of reaching out for help brings up a particular shame, the sense that needing it means you've failed at handling yourself, this chapter is for you.

Here is the principle. Needing help isn't a failure of the work you've done. It's often the wisest next step in it. Some of the most important parts of this material are genuinely better done with a trained person beside you, not because you're broken, but because certain things, the deepest things, are nearly impossible to reach alone. Reaching out isn't the opposite of self-reliance. It's what self-reliance does when it's honest about its own limits.

Help Is Not a Failure

The shame around getting help, for people with this pattern, is specific and worth naming.

It isn't only the general stigma that still hangs around therapy, though that exists. It's that the defectiveness belief has a particular stake here. If you go to a professional and let them see you, fully, that's the most exposed you can possibly be, to the exact kind of judgment the belief most fears, from the exact kind of person whose assessment would seem most authoritative. The belief will fight reaching out harder than almost anything, because a therapist's chair is the belief's worst-case scenario, being truly seen by an expert in seeing.

So the shame isn't a sign you don't need help. It's often a sign you've found the place the pattern least wants you to go, which is frequently the place that would help most.

Let me say the reframe directly. Reaching out for help is not an admission that the self-help failed. The reading you've done isn't lessened by deciding the next steps are better taken with company. Self-help and professional help aren't rivals. They're a sequence, and a wise one. Many people read their way to the edge of what reading can do, and then, sensibly, find a person to go further with. That's not failure. That's good navigation of your own progress.

Felix had done real work alone. The therapy didn't erase that work; it built on it. He walked into that office further along than he'd have been with no books at all, and the therapist could start from there. The self-help and the therapy were on the same side.

Signs It Might Be Time

You don't need a crisis to deserve help. That's worth saying first, because many people with this pattern wait until things are unbearable, on the theory that anything less doesn't qualify. It does qualify. You're allowed to get help for a life that's working but smaller than it should be, not only for a life that's falling apart.

That said, here are some signs that reaching out might be the right next step. If you've been doing the work and keep hitting a layer you can't get past alone, the way Felix did. If the material around your younger self, from Chapter 7, brings up more than you can hold by yourself. If the pattern is costing you something you care about badly enough that you don't want to leave the outcome to slow self-directed progress. If you've noticed your mood sinking in a way that goes beyond the pattern itself. If you're more alone than is safe, and the isolation has started to feel dangerous rather than merely sad.

That last one matters most. If you ever reach a point where the distress feels like more than you can carry, please don't wait for it to qualify as bad enough. Reach out then, to a professional, a doctor, a trusted person, or your local emergency or crisis services. There's a short, supportive note about this in the back of the book. You don't have to be in crisis to get help, and if you are near one, you especially don't have to manage it alone.

What Therapy Actually Offers

For readers who've never been, therapy can be a vague and slightly intimidating idea, so let me demystify it.

Good therapy, for this pattern, offers a few things a book can't. It offers a real relationship in which to do the work of being seen, which means the very thing you're afraid of becomes the thing you get to practice, safely, with someone trained to make it survivable. It offers a witness for the parts of you that have been alone too long, especially the younger self, who often can't be reached without another steady person in the room. It offers someone who can hold the material when it gets bigger than you can hold by yourself, so you're not doing the deepest work without a net. And it offers an outside view, someone who can see the pattern from a vantage point you can't occupy from inside it.

Therapy is not someone telling you what's wrong with you. Good therapy is closer to the opposite. It's someone helping you see what happened to you, with you, on your side, at a pace you can manage.

There's a particular thing therapy can do for this pattern that's worth naming, because it's the whole point. The pattern was built in relationships, early ones, where being seen wasn't safe. It heals, in large part, in a relationship too, a new one, where being seen turns out to be safe after all. A therapist who stays, week after week, who sees the parts of you that you were sure would drive someone away, and who doesn't leave, is offering a slow correction to the original lesson. The correction isn't delivered in words. It's delivered in the steady fact of someone seeing you and staying. That's something a book, however useful, structurally cannot give you. A book can't stay in the room. A person can, and the staying is the medicine.

The Approaches That Help

There are several kinds of therapy that help with these patterns, and you don't need to become an expert. A plain map is enough.

Schema therapy is the approach this book has drawn on throughout. It was built specifically for the deep, early patterns we've been discussing, the schemas and the modes, the critic and the wall and the younger self. It works directly with those parts and with the unmet needs underneath them. For many people with this pattern, it may be a strong fit because it was designed for enduring schemas and coping modes. The broader evidence base supports schema therapy for several personality-disorder presentations, while AVPD-specific treatment research remains smaller and still developing (Bachrach & Arntz, 2021; Bamelis et al., 2014; Lampe & Malhi, 2018).

Cognitive behavioral therapy works with the thoughts and behaviors that keep the pattern running. It tends to be more structured and present-focused. It can be very helpful, especially for the more visible layers, the social anxiety and the avoidance behaviors, though some people find it reaches the surface more readily than the depth.

Acceptance and commitment therapy, which we drew on in the last chapter, helps you act on your values while making room for difficult feelings rather than waiting for them to disappear. Psychodynamic and other depth approaches work, often over longer periods, with the early relationships and unconscious patterns that shaped you.

You don't have to pick the perfect one before you start. A good therapist of almost any of these orientations, who you feel safe with, is worth more than the theoretically ideal approach delivered by someone you don't click with. The relationship matters more than the brand. Start with what's available and what feels right, and adjust if you need to.

What the First Few Sessions Feel Like

People imagine the first session as a kind of exposure, walking in and being asked to bare everything. It almost never works that way.

The first session or two is mostly practical and gentle. The therapist asks what brings you in. You say as much or as little as you're ready to. They ask about your history at a level you control. Nobody makes you relive anything. A good therapist spends the early sessions building enough safety that the harder work becomes possible later, which means the start is usually slower and kinder than people fear. You're allowed to go at your pace. You're allowed to say you're not ready to talk about something. You're allowed, in fact, to spend a whole early session just talking about how strange and hard it is to be there.

Felix's first session was, by his account, almost disappointingly ordinary. He'd braced for an excavation. What he got was a calm conversation in which he said roughly what had brought him, the therapist listened in a way he wasn't used to being listened to, and they agreed to meet again. The relief wasn't from any breakthrough. It was from discovering that the thing he'd feared for years was, in practice, survivable and even kind.

How to Look for a Therapist

In plain terms, here's how people find a therapist, without me sending you to any particular service.

You can ask your doctor, who can often point you toward local options or referrals. You can search professional directories, the registers kept by the bodies that license and regulate therapists in your country, which let you filter by location, approach, and what they work with. You can ask people you trust, if you have anyone who's been, since personal recommendation is often how people find someone good. If you have any kind of employee assistance program or student counseling service, those are doors in too.

When you look, you can search for the approach if you want one in particular. The word *schema therapy* will find practitioners trained in it. So will *therapist for avoidant patterns* or simply a good general therapist who works with anxiety, self-esteem, and relationships. You don't need the perfect search term. You need a qualified, regulated person you can start with.

One practical note. It's normal, and wise, to have a first conversation with a prospective therapist before committing, sometimes a short free call, to get a feel for whether you'd feel safe with them. Feeling safe with the person matters more than their credentials on paper, within the bounds of them being properly qualified and regulated. Trust that instinct.

Bringing This Book Along

If you do start working with someone, you're welcome to bring what you've learned here with you. The language of this book, the quiet distance, the belief, the critic, the wall, the younger you, can give you a head start in describing your own experience to a therapist.

There's also a companion to this book written for clinicians, the Clinician's Manual version of this same material. If your therapist is curious about the specific schema therapy framework this book draws on, that volume lays it out in professional terms. You don't need it yourself; this book is the one written for you. But it exists, and a therapist you're working with might find it a useful map of the approach you've already been learning from the inside.

A Readiness Reflection

Here is the first reflection.

Ask yourself, gently and without pressure, a few questions. What would I want help with, if I let myself want it? What's the layer I keep reaching and backing away from alone? What am I afraid a therapist would think, and is that fear the pattern talking? If nothing changed for another five years, how would I feel about that?

You don't have to act on the answers. You're just letting yourself notice whether some part of you has been wanting this and not allowing the want. Naming the want, as we practiced in Chapter 9, is itself a step.

Questions to Ask a Therapist

Here is the second reflection, for if you do reach out.

It's reasonable to ask a prospective therapist a few things before you start. What approach do they use, and have they worked with patterns like avoidance, social anxiety, and low self-worth? How do they tend to work in the early sessions? What does the practical side look like, frequency, length, cost? And, mostly, you're listening underneath the answers for onc thing, whether you feel a little safer talking to this person than you expected to. That feeling is data worth trusting.

One Step Toward Support

Your action, if you want it, is one concrete step toward support. A small one counts.

It doesn't have to be booking a session. It can be looking at a directory for ten minutes. Asking your doctor at your next appointment. Mentioning to one trusted person that you've been thinking about it. Saving the name of one therapist who looks like a possible fit. The step is small on purpose, because the pattern will fight the large version hardest. One small step toward support, taken because some part of you wants the help, is the whole assignment, and only if you want it.

In a Nutshell

Needing help isn't a failure of the work you've done. It's often the wisest next step, because the deepest layers are nearly impossible to reach alone. The shame around reaching out is the pattern protecting its worst-case scenario, being truly seen by an expert, which is frequently a sign you've found the place that would help most. You don't need a crisis to deserve help. Good therapy offers a relationship in which to practice being seen, a witness for the parts that have been alone too long, and someone to hold the material when it gets big. Several approaches help, schema therapy among them, but the relationship matters more than the brand. Find a qualified person you feel a little safer with than you expected. Take one small step toward support this week, if you want it.

Conclusion

When Ines started this work, she left a leaving-drinks early, stood at the edge of the room, and went home before anyone noticed she'd gone. You met her in those first pages. A woman who longed for the warmth in the room and could not let herself walk into it.

I want to tell you where people like Ines tend to end up, not because change is guaranteed, and not because the ending is tidy, but because you've come a long way through this book and you deserve an honest picture of what the work adds up to.

It does not add up to a cure. There's no version of this where you wake up one morning and the pattern is gone, the fear is absent, and you're a naturally outgoing person who can't remember what the quiet distance felt like. That person doesn't exist, and chasing them is its own kind of trap. What the work adds up to is something quieter and more durable. The pattern loosens. The grip eases. The distance between what you want and what you let yourself have narrows, year by year, until one day you notice you're living closer to the center of your own life than you ever used to.

What You Have Now

Look at what you're carrying out of this book.

You understand the pattern. You can see the quiet distance for what it is, a learned way of staying safe that costs you the closeness you most want. You know it isn't a flaw in your character. It's a strategy, built young, that has outlived the situation it was built for.

You've met its parts. The belief that runs the show, the one that says you're not, in some hard to name way, enough. The critic that delivers the belief's lines in your own voice. The wall that goes up to protect you. And the younger you, still in there, who did the original work of surviving and has been waiting a long time for someone to come back for them.

You have tools. The naming. The kinder sentence. The grounding pause. The small experiments, run with curiosity rather than endured as ordeals. The repair that matters more than the rupture. The values that let you act while afraid. The maintenance plan for the bad weeks. None of these is a magic trick. All of them are real, and they work the way real things work, slowly, with repetition, in a direction.

And you know where to turn if you want more. The work that's better done with a witness, and how to find one, without shame.

Change Is a Direction, Not a Finish Line

Here is the thing I most want you to take with you.

Change, in this work, is a direction, not a finish line. You will not arrive. There's no day when you're done. What there is, instead, is a heading you've chosen, and a thousand small chances, every week, to move a little further along it. Some weeks you'll move forward. Some weeks you'll slip back. The slipping back isn't failure; it's weather, and you know now how to wait it out with kindness rather than collapse.

The measure of this work was never going to be whether you stopped being afraid. The measure is whether, over time, your life gets larger. Whether you sit a little closer to the front of the room. Whether you send the message before the push can stop you. Whether you let one more person see one more true thing. Whether the talent comes out of the spare room. Whether you go back, after you withdraw, and say the honest thing. Each of these is small. Together, across years, they're a different life.

An Invitation to Keep Going Gently

So this isn't really an ending. It's a handing-over. The book stops here. The work continues, in your hands now, at your pace.

Go gently. The pattern was built by harshness, and it will not be undone by more of it. Be as kind to yourself in this work as you'd be to someone you loved who was trying as hard as you are. When you slip, treat it as weather. When you move forward, let it count, and don't let the old belief downgrade it. When it gets too big to carry alone, reach for help, and let that be a sign of wisdom rather than weakness.

Ines, these days, still feels the pull to leave the room early. The fear didn't vanish. What changed is that more often now, she stays. She walks into the warmth she used to watch from the edge. She's afraid when she does it, and she does it anyway, because she decided that the warmth mattered more than the fear. That's not a cure. It's better than a cure. It's a life, lived at something much closer to full volume, by someone who used to live at the edge of the room.

You can have that too. Not perfectly. Not all at once. But in the direction you're now heading, one small, brave, ordinary step at a time.

Keep going. Gently. You've already begun.

Your Pattern Map

A single page to pull the book together. You can fill this in lightly, in pencil, and change it as you learn more about yourself. It's a map, not a verdict.

The belief underneath. In your own words, the sentence the pattern runs on. The thing it says you are, in some hard to name way. Write the version that's true for you, the one you caught yourself saying back in Chapter 3.

Where it shows up most. The two or three settings where you hold back most reliably. Work. Friendship. Love. Family. The ordinary moments. Mark yours, from Chapter 1.

The parts of you. Your critic, and what it tends to say. Your wall, and how it shows up, going quiet, going numb, disappearing, the screen. And the younger you, the part that learned to hide, who you began to meet in Chapter 7.

Your steadier responses. Next to each part, the response you're learning. To the critic, the kinder sentence. To the wall, naming it as it rises and the grounding pause. To the younger you, the few kind sentences and the small returns.

The directions you've chosen. The two or three values from Chapter 13. What you're moving toward, not just what you're moving away from. The answer to give the fear when it asks why you'd do something uncomfortable.

Keep this page where you'll see it. When a hard moment comes and you can't think clearly, this is the map back.

The Self-Compassion Toolkit

A short menu for hard moments. You don't need all of these. Pick the one or two that fit the moment you're in.

The friend question. Ask what you'd say to someone you loved who was in exactly your situation, and say that to yourself. You already have a kind voice. This points it inward.

A hand and a breath. Put a hand on your chest or your arm. Take one slow breath. Physical warmth, even your own, signals safety to the part of you that's braced. You don't have to believe in it for it to do something.

Name the critic. When the harsh voice starts, name it. *That's the critic.* The naming puts you outside the voice, watching it, rather than inside it, obeying.

Common humanity. Remind yourself that whatever you're ashamed of, struggling, failing, falling short, is one of the most universal human experiences there is. You're not failing at being a person. You're doing the human thing, which includes this.

The sober kind sentence. Not a pep talk. The accurate, friend-sized version of what actually happened. The one the critic isn't letting into the room.

One kind thing on purpose. Do one small thing that treats you as someone worth treating well, and let yourself notice you're doing it. Not a reward you earned. A kindness given freely.

Use these the way you'd use anything in a toolkit. Reach for the one that fits. Put it down when you're done.

Connection Experiments

A reader-paced menu of small steps toward being seen. These are experiments, not ordeals. You run them out of curiosity about what happens, not to prove you can endure them. Pick ones you choose, at a size you can actually imagine doing. Build your own ladder from the lower rungs up.

Lower rungs, smaller risk. Answer *how are you* with one true sentence. Say a real opinion in a conversation where you'd normally stay neutral. Leave something you made visible instead of putting it away. Greet a neighbor or learn a barista's name. Send one small message you'd normally talk yourself out of.

Middle rungs. Show one thing you made to one person whose response matters to you. Ask one person one question you'd normally swallow. Sit with the group instead of alone, once. Say the idea in the meeting before someone else says a worse version. Tell one person one true thing about how you actually are.

Higher rungs, when you're ready. Apply for the thing. Lead the thing. Show the work more widely. Have the honest conversation you've been avoiding. Let someone all the way in on something that matters.

After each experiment, debrief kindly. What did you actually do? What actually happened, compared to what you feared would happen? What did you learn? Write it down if you can. Over time, the record of what actually happens becomes the strongest evidence you have against the old belief, because the belief keeps predicting disasters that mostly don't arrive.

Rank your own rungs. Nobody else knows which acts of visibility cost you what. Climb only as fast as the climbing stays survivable.

Your Maintenance Plan

A short template to fill in while the weather is clear, for the version of you who'll be having a hard week and won't be able to think clearly. Copy it somewhere you'll find it.

What this is all for. My chosen directions, the two or three values I'm moving toward. When I'm struggling, this is why the work matters.

My three earliest warning signs. The very first signs that I'm sliding back, not the late ones. For many people these are small: sleeping worse, cancelling things, letting messages sit, a particular tightness returning, the screen coming out more, quietly retreating from people. Mine are:

One.

Two.

Three.

My kind response to each. Not a telling-off. A gentle plan. For each warning sign, what I'll do when I notice it, said the way I'd say it to a friend.

What reliably helps me. The two or three things I've learned actually work for me. The grounding pause. Reaching out to a specific person. A particular walk. Whatever I know helps.

The reminder. A bad week is weather, not a verdict. It tells me about today's conditions, not about my worth or my whole life. It will pass. I've come back before, and I can come back again.

Finding Help

Plain guidance, and a supportive note for anyone in real distress.

If you'd like to work with someone, there are several straightforward doors in. Your doctor can often point you toward local options or referrals. The professional directories kept by the bodies that license and regulate therapists in your country let you search by location and approach, and confirm that someone is properly qualified. People you trust who've been to therapy are often the best source of a recommendation. Employee assistance programs and student counseling services, if you have access to them, are doors in too.

When you search, you can look for a particular approach if you want one. The term *schema therapy* will find practitioners trained in the framework this book draws on. A good general therapist who works with anxiety, self-worth, and relationships is also a fine place to start. It's normal and wise to have a short first conversation with a prospective therapist before committing, to sense whether you feel safe with them. That feeling matters.

A note for harder moments. If you're in real distress right now, please don't wait until it feels bad enough to qualify. You deserve support before things reach a crisis, and especially if they have. Reach out to someone you trust, contact your doctor, or contact your local emergency services or a crisis line in your area. If you're somewhere you can't keep yourself safe, treat that as the emergency it is and reach for immediate help. You don't have to carry the heaviest moments alone, and reaching out in them is not weakness. It's the bravest and wisest thing a person can do.

Further Reading

If you want to go further, a few directions.

This book has a companion written for clinicians, a Clinician's Manual covering the same schema therapy approach in professional terms. You don't need it; this book is the one written for you. But if you're working with a therapist who's curious about the specific framework here, that volume maps the approach in clinical language, and you're welcome to point them to it.

Beyond that, the ideas in this book draw on a body of work you can explore at your own pace. The schema therapy framework, the research on self-compassion, the values-based approach to acting while afraid, and the literature on avoidant patterns more broadly are all available in fuller form for readers who want the deeper background. The references at the end of each chapter point the way.

Mostly, though, the further reading that matters now isn't more reading. It's the slow, gentle practice of what you already have. The book stops here. The work is yours, at your pace, in the direction you've chosen. Go gently, and keep going.

References

Arntz, A., & Weertman, A. (1999). Treatment of childhood memories: Theory and practice. Behaviour Research and Therapy, 37(8), 715-740. https://doi.org/10.1016/S0005-7967(98)00173-9

Bachrach, N., & Arntz, A. (2021). Group schema therapy for patients with cluster-C personality disorders: A case study on avoidant personality disorder. Journal of Clinical Psychology, 77(5), 1233-1248. https://doi.org/10.1002/jclp.23118

Bamelis, L. L. M., Evers, S. M. A. A., Spinhoven, P., & Arntz, A. (2014). Results of a multicenter randomized controlled trial of the clinical effectiveness of schema therapy for personality disorders. The American Journal of Psychiatry, 171(3), 305-322. https://doi.org/10.1176/appi.ajp.2013.12040518

Clark, D. M., & Wells, A. (1995). A cognitive model of social phobia. In R. G. Heimberg, M. R. Liebowitz, D. A. Hope, & F. R. Schneier (Eds.), Social phobia: Diagnosis, assessment, and treatment (pp. 69-93). Guilford Press.

Eubanks, C. F., Muran, J. C., & Safran, J. D. (2018). Alliance rupture repair: A meta-analysis. Psychotherapy, 55(4), 508-519. https://doi.org/10.1037/pst0000185

Gilbert, P. (2009). The compassionate mind: A new approach to life's challenges. Constable.

Grant, B. F., Hasin, D. S., Stinson, F. S., Dawson, D. A., Chou, S. P., Ruan, W. J., & Pickering, R. P. (2004). Prevalence, correlates, and disability of personality disorders in the United States: Results from the National Epidemiologic Survey on Alcohol and Related Conditions. The Journal of Clinical Psychiatry, 65(7), 948-958.

Hayes, S. C., Strosahl, K. D., & Wilson, K. G. (2012). Acceptance and commitment therapy: The process and practice of mindful change (2nd ed.). Guilford Press.

Hull, L., Petrides, K. V., Allison, C., Smith, P., Baron-Cohen, S., Lai, M.-C., & Mandy, W. (2017). "Putting on my best normal": Social camouflaging in adults with autism spectrum conditions. Journal of Autism and Developmental Disorders, 47(8), 2519-2534. https://doi.org/10.1007/s10803-017-3166-5

Kentrou, V., Livingston, L. A., Grove, R., Hoekstra, R. A., & Begeer, S. (2024). Perceived misdiagnosis of psychiatric conditions in autistic adults. eClinicalMedicine, 71, Article 102586. https://doi.org/10.1016/j.eclinm.2024.102586

Lampe, L., & Malhi, G. S. (2018). Avoidant personality disorder: Current insights. Psychology Research and Behavior Management, 11, 55-66. https://doi.org/10.2147/PRBM.S121073

Najavits, L. M. (2002). Seeking safety: A treatment manual for PTSD and substance abuse. Guilford Press.

Neff, K. D. (2003). Self-compassion: An alternative conceptualization of a healthy attitude toward oneself. Self and Identity, 2(2), 85-101. https://doi.org/10.1080/15298860309032

Tillfors, M., Furmark, T., Ekselius, L., & Fredrikson, M. (2004). Social phobia and avoidant personality disorder: One spectrum disorder? Nordic Journal of Psychiatry, 58(2), 147-152. https://doi.org/10.1080/08039480410005530

Trull, T. J., Jahng, S., Tomko, R. L., Wood, P. K., & Sher, K. J. (2010). Revised NESARC personality disorder diagnoses: Gender, prevalence, and comorbidity with substance dependence disorders. Journal of Personality Disorders, 24(4), 412-426. https://doi.org/10.1521/pedi.2010.24.4.412

Wilberg, T., Pedersen, G., Bremer, K., Johansen, M. S., & Kvarstein, E. H. (2023). Combined group and individual therapy for patients with avoidant personality disorder: A pilot study. Frontiers in Psychiatry, 14, Article 1181686. https://doi.org/10.3389/fpsyt.2023.1181686

Young, J. E., Klosko, J. S., & Weishaar, M. E. (2003). Schema therapy: A practitioner's guide. Guilford Press.

www.ingramcontent.com/pod-product-compliance
Lightning Source LLC
LaVergne TN
LVHW022050200926
848481LV00003B/855
9781764726528